T0013625

 # Nova Scotia's Historic Inland Communities

NOVA SCOTIA'S HISTORIC INLAND COMMUNITIES

The Gathering Places and Settlements that Shaped the Province

JOAN DAWSON

NIMBUS
PUBLISHING
— NIMBUS.CA —

Copyright © 2022, Joan Dawson

All rights reserved. No part of this book may be reproduced, stored in a retrieval system or transmitted in any form or by any means without the prior written permission from the publisher, or, in the case of photocopying or other reprographic copying, permission from Access Copyright, 1 Yonge Street, Suite 1900, Toronto, Ontario M5E 1E5.

Nimbus Publishing Limited
3660 Strawberry Hill Street, Halifax, NS, B3K 5A9
(902) 455-4286 nimbus.ca

Printed and bound in Canada

NB1573

Design: Jenn Embree
Editor: Paula Sarson
Cover image: Bear River postcard, collection of Dan Soucoup

Library and Archives Canada Cataloguing in Publication

Title: Nova Scotia's historic inland communities : the gathering places and
   settlements that shaped the province / Joan Dawson.
Names: Dawson, Joan, 1932- author.
Description: Series statement: Shaping Nova Scotia | Includes
   bibliographical references.
Identifiers: Canadiana (print) 20210379219 | Canadiana (ebook) 20210379243
   ISBN 9781774710623 (softcover)
   ISBN 9781774710791 (EPUB)
Subjects: LCSH: Nova Scotia—History. | LCSH: Cities and towns—Nova Scotia—
   History. | LCSH: Community life—Nova Scotia—History.
Classification: LCC FC2311 .D39 2022 | DDC 971.6—dc23

Nimbus Publishing acknowledges the financial support for its publishing activities from the Government of Canada, the Canada Council for the Arts, and from the Province of Nova Scotia. We are pleased to work in partnership with the Province of Nova Scotia to develop and promote our creative industries for the benefit of all Nova Scotians.

To all victims of colonialism, past and present

TABLE OF CONTENTS

Kentville, Nova Scotia.

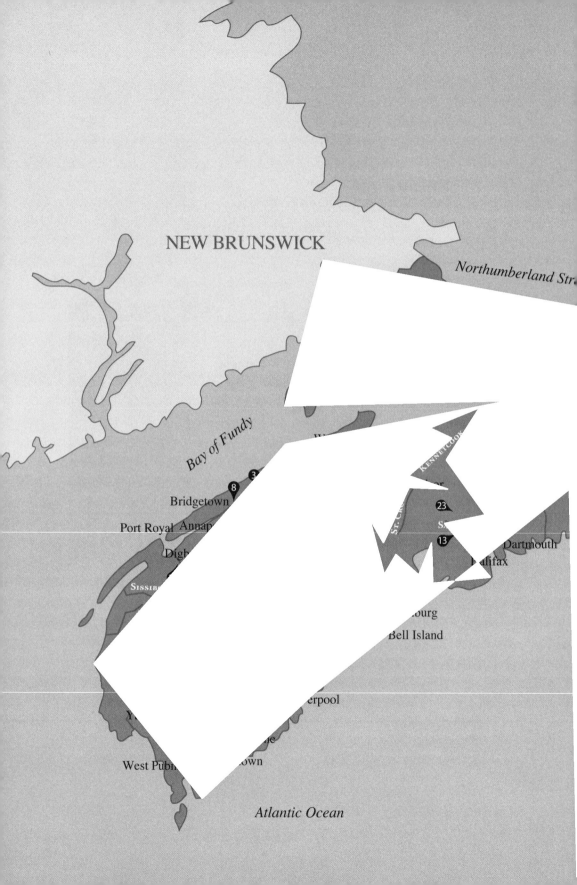

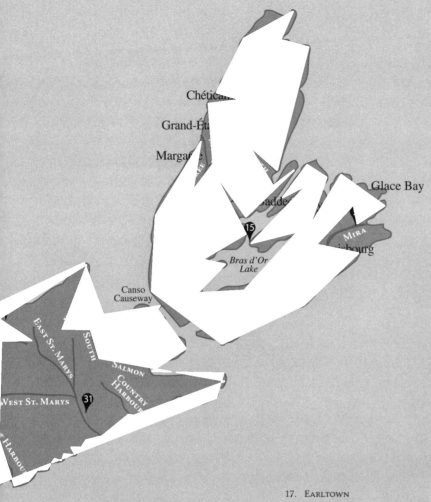

Chéticamp

Grand-Étang

Margaree

Glace Bay

Baddeck

Mira

ichbourg

Bras d'Or
Lake

15

Canso
Causeway

EAST ST. MARYS

SOUTH

SALMON

COUNTRY HARBOUR

WEST ST. MARYS

31

HARBOUR

Bear River, Nova Scotia.

PREFACE

———— ≋ ————

Like many Nova Scotians, I live near the sea, and most of my journeys take me to other coastal communities. Tourists in Nova Scotia also tend to follow seaside routes, in search of beaches, shoreline vistas, and traces of our maritime history. But our often overlooked inland and cross-country roads run alongside scenic lakes and rivers, forests and farmlands, and through communities that were established far from the ocean as people gradually discovered resources in the interior from which they could make a living. Land agents like Alexander McNutt acquired large tracts of land, which they encouraged settlers to develop. Trunks 1 and 2, the oldest roads in the province, were the only two "great roads" in Nova Scotia in the early nineteenth century. These roads ran across the peninsula and linked the capital of Halifax with Windsor and Truro respectively. Today, they pass through some of the oldest historic inland communities in Nova Scotia. Originally, these routes were of strategic and commercial importance, and as roads were developed, they also opened the way for roadside property removed from the coast to be granted to would-be settlers.

Some of these communities remained small and scattered, while others evolved into thriving industrial or commercial centres. They have all experienced significant changes and over the years have had to adapt with new technologies in order to prosper. In my travels, I have found derelict mills that were once the basis of their communities' economy, and gracious old homes that reflect the prosperity of former residents. Place names sometimes suggest interesting origins—why would a community be called Blockhouse or Paradise? I set out to research some of these places and found that although they are less well known as tourist destinations, many inland communities have fascinating histories that contribute to Nova Scotia as we know it today.

INTRODUCTION

---≈---

When the Europeans first crossed the Atlantic Ocean, the Mi'kmaq were travelling freely across the interior of their territory called Mi'kma'ki. The story of Nova Scotia's inland communities begins with them. For thousands of years after the last vestiges of the Laurentide Ice Sheet retreated from the place we call Nova Scotia, the land was covered in dense forest. In its shelter lived generations of Indigenous peoples, who dwelled here long before Europeans arrived. They were equally at home in the interior and on the coast of Mi'kma'ki. These hunter-gatherers harvested from nature only what they needed and left little or no trace of their wanderings. Although they were mainly nomadic, the Mi'kmaq established traditional gathering places, which had spiritual or economic significance and became seasonal, sometimes permanent, communities. In winter they hunted in the interior for animals that provided meat for food, fur for clothing, bone and sinew for tools and other objects. The rivers and lakes supplied fish. The forest supplied berries and medicinal herbs, and materials for the wigwams in which they sheltered and for their birchbark canoes. Each spring and fall, they travelled in these canoes downriver to the shore.

By contrast, early French and British settlers rarely penetrated far inland and instead clustered around the harbours that sheltered their fishing vessels and trading ships. They ventured into the forest only to cut wood for shelter and fuel.

As more settlers arrived looking for land in what would become the province, opportunities for inland development increased, and communities grew up along roads and rivers farther from the sea. The Acadians created the first European inland communities toward the end of the seventeenth century, establishing small villages of families and friends when they dyked and drained marshlands along the Annapolis River and the rivers draining into the Minas Basin. These Acadian villages did not impede Mi'kmaw hunting and fishing, and newcomers of French origin were frequently helped by their Indigenous neighbours, who shared with them their survival skills. The two populations became friends and allies.

The British gained permanent control of Nova Scotia in the early eighteenth century but did not begin to introduce settlers until the 1749 founding of a new capital at Halifax. The colonial officials' contemptuous attitudes and disregard for the First Nations' sacred sites and ways of life immediately aroused resentment and provoked animosity among the Mi'kmaq, who retaliated against British brutality, resulting in raids and skirmishes. For many years, these conflicts discouraged settlers from venturing far from the capital or from the new town of Lunenburg, established in 1753 for Protestant settlers from Germany, France, and Switzerland. After Peace and Friendship Treaties were signed between the opposing factions in 1760 and '61, residents began to venture inland, shifting their economic focus from fishing and shipbuilding to agriculture and commercial endeavours.

The Expulsion of 1755 left vacant the Acadian farmlands along the Bay of Fundy and the rivers flowing into it until the 1760s, when Governor Lawrence brought in colonists from New England to repopulate the abandoned settlements and revive agriculture. Townships were laid out by the colonial government to replace the former Acadian parishes, and the newcomers, known as Planters, began to arrive. They were provided with town lots on the coast and farm lots that spread inland, where some families began to form communities. Not all the original grantees took up their lots, which were often acquired by their neighbours to increase their holdings.

In the early 1780s, after the American Revolution, a flood of Loyalist settlers, who preferred to remain under British rule, arrived in Nova Scotia. Some joined their countrymen in existing communities, while others were granted land in a series of new townships in places like Digby and Shelburne. The end of the war also left some former soldiers in Nova Scotia. They, too, were offered land.

Among the Loyalists were a number of "Free Blacks," former slaves who had fought alongside the British and were promised freedom and land as a reward. A second wave of Black immigrants were former slaves who were brought against their will from Jamaica, where they had escaped from plantations and rebelled against efforts to recapture them. Many of these groups seized the first opportunity to leave Nova Scotia, but a third contingent, the so-called Chesapeake Blacks, came with returning troops after the War of 1812 and remained here.

Highland Scots, evicted by their landlords to make room for pasturing sheep in what were known as the Clearances, came to make a fresh start here in the late eighteenth century. Additional settlers from Britain were slow to come to Nova Scotia until the nineteenth century. At this time, large-scale immigration took place, partly on account of poverty in sectors of Britain, including the Scottish Highlands where families were still being evicted from their homes to devote more land for sheep.

Many Nova Scotia inland communities can trace their origins to this period. Much of the arable land along the coast and lower reaches of the rivers was already claimed, and newcomers travelled up the rivers and along trails farther inland in search of suitable places to create small farms. Initially, these farms may have been scattered over a wide area, but eventually, communities grew up where schools, churches, stores, and other services were established. After the War of 1812, the colonial government again offered land to disbanded soldiers and created new communities in previously undeveloped inland areas.

The trails between early settlements were rough, but roads as we know them began to develop in the early nineteenth century. The two "great roads," from Halifax to Windsor and from Halifax to Truro, were key to the development of commerce and encouraged granting of roadside property away from the coast to would-be settlers.

Once the colonial government realized the potential of inland areas for lumbering and farming, surveying crews made their way through the woods with compasses, rods, and chains to blaze routes for the construction of new roads intended to open areas for development. When a road was established, would-be settlers eyed potential properties and sought grants from the Crown, which in early days were conditional on recipients clearing and developing their property. Failure to comply resulted in the land being escheated to the government for re-granting to a new owner. Communities grew up where land was most fertile. Subsistence farming was often supplemented by logging.

As these communities became established, they attracted skilled tradesmen like blacksmiths who maintained farm equipment and livestock, and carpenters who supplied material for housing and developed more specialized trades like the building and repair of carriages and buggies. Forests were a valuable source of lumber, and sawmills were set up wherever water power was readily available. The same brooks often powered gristmills. Storekeepers brought in supplies from merchants on the coast. Clergy and teachers arrived to set up churches and schools, and populations grew.

Another natural resource that became important in the nineteenth century was mineral wealth, which sparked the development of industrial towns. People had been aware of the existence of coal since it was used in Louisbourg in the mid-eighteenth century, but it was not commercially exploited on a large scale until a major company, the General Mining Association, was granted exclusive mining rights in Nova Scotia in 1827. Workers were housed in company towns and provided with basic amenities. The economy of other communities relied on iron ore deposits. Hundreds of immigrants came to Nova Scotia during the nineteenth century in response to a need for workers in these developing industries. In the 1860s, gold was found in several areas, which launched Nova Scotia's gold rush; however, this resource was limited, and the boom towns that sprang up almost overnight often disappeared just as quickly.

The prosperity of many communities peaked toward the end of the nineteenth century and then declined during the twentieth as businesses on which their economies were based were unable to compete with bigger enterprises in larger centres. Some communities struggled to survive, while a few maintained the industries that employed their population well into the twentieth century. By the opening of the present century, many village stores, schools, and churches had closed, and people were driving to nearby towns for goods and services and for employment. Today's most successful inland communities have endured because entrepreneurs have adapted to changing circumstances by developing new businesses able to revive faltering economies. Regardless of their current state, Nova Scotia's inland communities have stories worth telling.

1

THE OLDEST COMMUNITIES

When Britain gained permanent control of Nova Scotia in 1713, there were already two groups of residents: the Mi'kmaq, who are counted among the Maritimes' earliest inhabitants, and the Acadians, who had arrived in the seventeenth century and by 1700 were moving inland. The British did not immediately bring in settlers, so these two groups formed the bulk of the population until the middle of the eighteenth century, when serious colonization began.

In the years following 1713, Britain finally achieved official control of Nova Scotia, but the garrison town of Annapolis Royal was the sole British settlement, while Acadian villages were scattered around the Bay of Fundy and its rivers. The Mi'kmaq continued to travel around their territories and meet in their traditional gathering places. Britain's hold on the colony evolved only gradually before 1760. This was a period of frequent conflict in Europe between the British and the French, and in Nova Scotia between the colonists and the Mi'kmaq. British authorities regarded the Acadian population as a threat to their stake—fearful that the Acadians would join with the Mi'kmaq in support of the French if they were to make any attempt to regain their former colony. To mitigate the perceived threat, Britain required the Acadians to swear an oath of allegiance to the Crown, which they did in 1730 only on condition that they would not be required to take up arms against the French or the Mi'kmaq. In the 1750s, the British rulers demanded that the Acadians' oath of allegiance be unconditional. The Acadians' insistence upon their original terms prompted the British response with the deportation of 1755.

MI'KMAW GATHERING PLACES

In the territory known as Mi'kma'ki, there were originally no permanent residential communities as we know them. The Indigenous inhabitants did not settle in one place year-round but moved seasonally between inland forests and coastal beaches, a testament to their symbiotic relationship with nature's seasons. There were, however, traditional gathering places where wigwams were set up year after year.

The Mi'kmaq residents welcomed and assisted the French settlers, with whom they became friends and allies. The newcomers included missionary priests, whose aim was to convert the Indigenous people to Christianity by setting up missions in their traditional gathering places. Although many of the Mi'kmaq accepted the priests' teachings, they retained their own spiritual values and their traditional way of life.

After the British Crown established its claim on Nova Scotia, British settlements, farms, and forestry activities increasingly encroached on Mi'kmaw territory. To define territorial boundaries for the Mi'kmaq as English communities expanded, the colonizing authorities created reserves that were only a fraction of the traditional Indigenous hunting grounds. This caused tremendous hardship as it limited the customary food supply. Mi'kmaw communities grew up on the reserves as residents began to plant crops and develop a more settled way of life.

Kejimkujik

Today, the national park and historic site familiarly known as "Keji" attracts visitors who enjoy camping and hiking and appreciate natural beauty. It is not a community as we understand the word now, but it has been populated, even if at times only seasonally, for thousands of years. Both Indigenous people and others have lived there from time to time. Visitors flock to the site today, and this protected area is still a spiritual home to many Mi'kmaq.

The park takes its name from Kejimkujik Lake, the largest of several in the area. Its official meaning, according to Parks Canada, is "tired muscles," though it is sometimes interpreted as "attempting to escape" or "swollen waters." The name's meaning given by the Mi'kmaw Place Names Digital Atlas is "little fairies," and the main lake was once known as Fairy Lake. The lake is fed by several rivers, and some smaller lakes are also linked to it by channels of water, but the main waterway, which served the Mi'kmaq as a major travel route across Mi'kma'ki, is the Mersey River, which flows out of the lake and runs southward through nearby Lake Rossignol to the Atlantic Ocean. The forests around Kejimkujik Lake served as winter quarters for many, and travellers on the Mersey pulled up their canoes on its shores.

Archaeologists have found evidence that Indigenous people have occupied the area around Kejimkujik Lake for as long as six thousand years. Here the bounty of the forest, the land, and the waters provided for the people's needs. Officially, according to Parks Canada's "A Mi'kmaw History," these early inhabitants are known as people of the Late Archaic tradition; later they were known as the Eastern Woodlands people, and today their successors are part of the Mi'kmaq First Nation.

The Mi'kmaq of Kejimkujik were semi-nomadic, until their way of life was impacted by European settlement. They spent late fall and winter in camps on the shores of the area's lakes and rivers, which were rich with freshwater fish. The forests around Kejimkujik Lake were prolific hunting grounds for moose and caribou. Nothing was wasted: the flesh provided food, the skins were used to make clothing, and the bones and sinew were used for tools and objects. One of the known Indigenous campsites, sometimes thought of as villages, was at Merrymakedge Beach, and two were at Eel Weir below George Lake. Eels were a staple food, and stone weirs were used to direct them and other fish to the place where they would be harvested. Spring found many Mi'kmaq paddling canoes down the Mersey to the coast, where they harvested molluscs in sandy estuaries.

The stories of the early Mi'kmaq were not recorded in words but were passed down orally through the generations. The past of these early inhabitants is also recorded in petroglyphs of which there is an impressive collection of about five hundred in Kejimkujik Park. These images carved on rocks depict both cultural and spiritual subjects. They show hunters, women in traditional costume with their distinctive cap, men with feather headdresses, birds, animals, fish, the canoes the Mi'kmaq travelled in, and the wigwams they lived in, as well as the sailing vessels that brought French and Basque fishers to the harbour at the mouth of the Mersey River. The images also include traditional Mi'kmaq spiritual symbols and crosses that reflect their conversion to Christianity. The number and variety of these petroglyphs indicate that this was a significant gathering place for centuries. Today, the site is protected and can be visited only with a guided tour.

The first written records we have of European contact with the Indigenous people of the Kejimkujik area are Samuel de Champlain's and Marc Lescarbot's accounts of a French expedition led in 1604 by Pierre Dugua de Monts, who had been granted a monopoly on the fur trade. The practice of trading manufactured goods for furs with the Mi'kmaq had developed from the time that European fishing vessels began to shelter in harbours along the Atlantic coast in the sixteenth century. In the seventeenth century, the French attempted to control the fur trade by granting rights to specific companies. The 1604 expedition arrived at the mouth of what is now the Mersey River, where they found a French fishing captain, Jean de Rossignol, illegally trading with the Mi'kmaq. Rossignol was taken prisoner and his vessel confiscated. The story goes that two of Rossignol's men escaped upriver with Mi'kmaw inhabitants, settled on the lake that would take Rossignol's name, and married Mi'kmaw women.

The first French communities, established in coastal areas in the seventeenth century, did not disturb the Mi'kmaq of Kejimkujik, who were probably surprised in the spring of 1686 to see three canoes entering the lake from the direction of Port Royal (now Annapolis Royal), carrying a party of Europeans along the traditional river route from the Annapolis Basin to the Atlantic Ocean. Mi'kmaw guides paddled these canoes, and the travellers included the intendant of New France, Jacques de Meulles, who had come from Quebec to inspect and report on the French colony of Acadie. The party probably spent a night camped on the shores of the lake before proceeding southward down the Mersey River to the Atlantic coast.

In the eighteenth century, European settlers introduced infectious diseases against which the Mi'kmaw inhabitants had no immunity, and so the illnesses spread rapidly, reducing the Mi'kmaw population. The general population around Kejimkujik Lake increased as British settlement expanded all across the province in the nineteenth century. Despite the Peace and Friendship Treaties they had signed with the British, the Mi'kmaq were forced off many of their traditional hunting grounds by newcomers logging and clearing land for farming. Some of the Indigenous inhabitants retreated to Kejimkujik, but it became increasingly difficult to maintain their traditional lifestyle. Poverty became rife.

When Joseph Howe was appointed Provincial Commissioner for Indian Affairs in 1842, he was determined to improve the conditions under which Nova Scotia's Mi'kmaw residents lived. According to Elder Daniel N. Paul, Howe probably saved them from extinction by encouraging them to adopt a more settled way of life, granting twelve parcels of land on Kejimkujik Lake to Mi'kmaw families to develop farms. Among these grantees was John Jeremy, whose name is preserved at Jeremys Bay. He and other members of the band cleared their land and established their homes beside the lake. They continued to hunt and fish, making use of the eel weirs as their ancestors had done.

Europeans also received grants and moved into the area in the early nineteenth century, but little of the land proved suitable for farming. Logging was more lucrative, and for a few years toward the end of the century, some gold mining also took place. The resident Mi'kmaq continued to depend as much on hunting and fishing as on farming. In the late 1800s, they increasingly made a living by working as guides to wealthy sportsmen from Canada, Britain, and the United States. Guiding remained a valuable source of income from the late nineteenth century to the early twentieth century.

The experience of visitors to Kejimkujik at this time is described vividly by Albert Bigelow Paine in his book *The Tent Dwellers*. In 1908, two well-to-do Americans, one experienced, the other—Paine—a novice, set out on a fishing trip with quantities of camping gear and two Mi'kmaw guides. Putting in at Jakes Landing, they paddled across Kejimkujik Lake and made their way through the series of smaller lakes to the Shelburne River and the Tobeatic area beyond. Paine describes the novelty of travelling in a birchbark canoe, camping, outdoor cooking, portaging, and generally adapting to the conditions of life on the lakes and in the woods. Not only did the guides show their guests the route and share their knowledge of the area's resources, but also they carried much of the gear on the portages.

A late nineteenth century Mi'kmaw camp.

As the area's popularity increased, lodges and cabins were built around the lake to accommodate visitors. In the second half of the twentieth century, the area took on a less commercial aspect as the Government of Canada designated it a National Park in 1969. It was recognized for its natural beauty, its abundant wildlife—some of it rare—and its cultural history as a traditional home of the Mi'kmaq. In 1995, the park was also designated a National Historic Site, honouring the thousands of years of Mi'kmaw presence there. Commemorative plaques were unveiled in 2000, followed by the establishment of a monument reflecting the shape of a traditional Mi'kmaw woman's cap. In 2010, the park was designated a Dark-Sky Preserve by the Royal Astronomical Society of Canada, restricting the use of artificial light and enabling skywatchers to enjoy clear views of moon, stars, and planets.

Today, Kejimkujik National Park and Historic Site welcomes visitors year-round, with hiking trails, campsites, guided tours, interpretive programs, and a wide range of facilities. It is no longer a residential community, but it remains a spiritual home to the Mi'kmaq, as well as a favourite recreational spot for Nova Scotians and for visitors from around the world.

Shubenacadie

A favourite summer adventure for many people is rafting with the tidal bore down the Shubenacadie River, whose turbulent waters carry them to the estuary. They may not be aware that the Mi'kmaq used the river for thousands of years as a major travel route across the peninsula from Halifax Harbour to the Bay of Fundy, by way of the Dartmouth lakes that were linked by portages. The name Shubenacadie comes from the Mi'kmaw name Sipekne'katik, meaning "abounding in groundnuts" or "where the wild potato grows." The name refers to a wide area of Mi'kmaw territory in central Nova Scotia through which the Shubenacadie River flows out of Grand Lake, and to the people who first lived there. Their descendants today are known as the Sipekne'katik First Nation.

At the end of the seventeenth century, Père Louis-Pierre Thury, a French missionary, planned to create a Mi'kmaw community at a central location in Sipekne'katik territory on the west side of the river, where he would introduce Christianity to the Indigenous inhabitants. In the early 1720s, a permanent mission dedicated to Saint Anne was established there by Père Antoine Gaulin from Quebec. He was followed in 1738 by the famous, or infamous, missionary Abbé Jean-Louis Le Loutre. Le Loutre had studied the Mi'kmaw language in Cape Breton before coming to Sipekne'katik and seems to have forged a close relationship with the Mi'kmaw parishioners, over whom he established considerable influence.

His first action after arriving was to oversee the construction of a chapel, identified later by British map-makers as a "Mass House" in the mission community. With the outbreak of King George's War between England and France in 1744, the community was also the base for Le Loutre's political activities: he attempted to persuade the Acadians to abandon their neutrality and rallied the Mi'kmaq inhabitants to harass British troops. The war ended with the first capture of Louisbourg by the British the following year.

Hostilities were renewed in 1749, with Mi'kmaw participation sparked by the establishment of Halifax on Indigenous territory. This time, Le Loutre succeeded in raising a militia of Acadian rebels led by Joseph "Beausoleil" Brossard that joined with Mi'kmaw warriors in guerrilla warfare against the British in what was known as Le Loutre's War. It was from the Sipekne'katik mission that the Mi'kmaq staged their attacks on Halifax and Dartmouth. As the war progressed, Le Loutre left the community for Chignecto, where French and British troops faced each other across the disputed border between Nova Scotia and the French territory north of the Missaguash River in what is now New Brunswick. Here Le Loutre would organize the Mi'kmaq to drive the innocent inhabitants of the Acadian village of Beaubassin on the British side into French territory and destroy the village to prevent British troops from finding food and shelter there.

After the French were defeated by the British in 1755, Le Loutre did not return to the Sipekne'katik mission but slipped away to Quebec and then to France. In 1760, the Sipekne'katik Mi'kmaq signed a treaty with the British authorities that brought an end to hostilities, at least for the time being.

In 1779, the lieutenant-governor of Nova Scotia, Michael Francklin, created a reserve, now known as the Indian Brook Reserve, on traditional Sipekne'katik territory. This gave the Mi'kmaq land rights but limited them to a meagre portion of their original terrain, and at some distance from the river. The more desirable riverside property now became available for white settlement. The new village of Shubenacadie was established amid potential farmland at the end of the eighteenth century. Farms were established on former Mi'kmaw hunting grounds, making it harder for the Indigenous inhabitants to eke out a living from the land.

During the nineteenth century, Shubenacadie village slowly grew. A schoolhouse built in 1805 replaced the private home where informal instruction was first given. Church services were held in a house or a barn until 1869, when the first Presbyterian church was built. While the chief occupations of the settlers were lumbering and farming, other trades and industries developed, particularly after the opening in 1841 of the post road from Halifax to Truro, which crossed the river at Shubenacadie by a covered bridge.

With the opening of the road, stagecoaches brought goods, mail, and passengers to the community, and livery stables provided travellers with horses for hire. Communications were further improved in 1858, when railway service came to Shubenacadie. Trains soon replaced the stagecoaches as the primary link to the capital. Famers sent their produce to market by rail, and industries became established: lumber was processed in the 1850s by James A. Pearson's steam-powered sawmill, and another steam mill run by Thomas Mitchell provided material for A. McLaughlin's adjacent shipyard.

The nineteenth century saw the revival in a new form of the traditional Mi'kmaw canoe route across the province, with the construction of the Shubenacadie Canal to bring vessels from Halifax Harbour through the Dartmouth lakes to the head of the Shubenacadie River. Canal construction began in the 1820s but proceeded slowly and with many delays. Finally, in the 1860s, freight traffic from Halifax came to Shubenacadie following this route; however, increasing use of the railway made the canal obsolete after only a few years.

By about 1870, when Ambrose Church was conducting surveys for his map of Hants County, Shubenacadie was a busy place. As well as the sawmill and shipyard, Church's business directory recorded a variety of businesses operating in the town. J. M. Nelson and A. Nelson were both running hotels, and two members of the Gass family were merchants, selling "dry goods, groceries, fancy notions, ready-made clothing, hats, caps, boots, shoes and rubbers, patent medicines, etc., etc." J. Gass also made saddles, harnesses, and trunks J. McDonald, a farmer, advertised "bricks always on hand," as did the brick manufacturers J. Miller & Co. There were carriage- and sleigh-makers, ships' carpenters, and, of course, farmers.

By the end of the century, dairy farmers in the area were sending milk in metal containers to Halifax by train. Watson Smith came to Shubenacadie in 1895 and set up shop in the former Orange Hall, where he made and repaired milk cans. The following year he put up a building of his own, and the business grew rapidly. His son Cullen ran a hardware store at the front of the building, and at the back was the tinsmith shop, where the elder Smith worked along with his other son, Harry. By 1942, over eighty thousand cream cans had been sold to Nova Scotia creameries. The hardware business expanded in the twentieth century and undertook plumbing and heating for some years. Today, the Watson Smith and Sons Tinsmith Shop and Hardware Store operates as a museum.

By the early twentieth century, the population of Shubenacadie had grown to about 850. There were stores and hotels, a shingle mill, a bank, post office and telegraph office, and four churches. Two serious fires, in 1930 and 1943 respectively, destroyed businesses, but rebuilding took place and the community recovered. Some of the fine nineteenth-century houses have survived, but many of the former businesses were no longer in operation by the later twentieth century.

These Mi'kmaw people were photographed at the Shubenacadie Reserve in 1927. Right to left: Joe Silliboy, Bayfield; Dr. Jeremiah Lonecloud, Millers Lake, Waverley; Louise Abram, Richibucto, NB, and her daughter, wife of Henry Sack, Truro.

In 1930, in accordance with federal government policy, the Shubenacadie Indian Residential School was established, run by the Catholic Church, and staffed by the Sisters of Charity. Mi'kmaw children from all over the Atlantic region were taken from their homes in an attempt to force assimilation through education. Some of these children were orphans, some were placed in the school by parents hoping to ensure their education, and others were forcibly removed from their homes. Education proved limited while discipline was harsh, corporal punishment was administered freely, food was poor, and accommodation was overcrowded, leading to the spread of diseases like tuberculosis, and even death. Children were forbidden to speak their native language, and any caught doing so suffered severe consequences. They were not allowed to return home, even for holidays, until the mid-1950s. Attempts to instill European-style culture into Indigenous children were supposedly intended to alleviate poverty among the Mi'kmaq, but the result was that generations of children were separated from their families, deprived of their language and culture, and abused in various ways until the school finally closed in 1967, leaving a legacy of trauma and alienation.

Eldon Pace launched a much more humane project in the late 1940s, when he opened a refuge for orphaned white-tailed deer on the far side of the river that later became the Shubenacadie Provincial Wildlife Park. The park opened in 1954 and has expanded into a major attraction for animal lovers. It is home to about ninety species of mammals and birds, many of which have been brought in injured and have been rehabilitated. It offers an ongoing education program and welcomes hundreds of schoolchildren each year. The wildlife park attracts many visitors and is the home of Shubenacadie Sam, the groundhog who emerges from his winter quarters on February 2 each year to "forecast" the weather for the rest of the season. If he sees his shadow, winter will continue for another six weeks. If not, Nova Scotians take it as an optimistic sign of an early spring.

Today, the community of Shubenacadie has a population of over two thousand. It remains the hub of the surrounding agricultural area, with its satellite provincial courthouse administered from Truro, its district school, and a variety of goods and services. The village welcomes tourists who come to visit Watson Smith's tinsmith shop, to go rafting, or just to view the tidal bore on the river.

ACADIAN/FRENCH ORIGINS

The French were the first to establish communities in the colony they called Acadie in the seventeenth century. The settlers, known as Acadians, created farms on marshlands on the Annapolis River and on the Minas Basin rivers by building dykes and aboiteaux, an effective drainage system they brought from western France. In Île Royale, which would later become known as Cape Breton Island, French farming communities grew up in the early eighteenth century to feed the population of the fortress town of Louisbourg. After the deportation and the destruction of Louisbourg, these former Acadian and French farmlands were taken over by British settlers who formed new communities.

Paradise

Paradise, situated on a bend in the Annapolis River between today's Bridgetown and Lawrencetown, is one of Nova Scotia's earliest recorded Acadian settlements. It appears on a map of the rivière du Port Royal (Annapolis River) made in 1684 by Sieur Jean de Laporte de Lalanne, a clerk in Louis XIV's département de la Marine. Lalanne was sent to Acadie that year to report on its timber supplies and its ports and harbours. While he was at Port Royal, he made an expedition upriver. His map shows buildings on the edge of marshland, on the north bank of the river, which he identifies as Paradis Terrestre ("earthly paradise").

The French were not the first people to come here. For thousands of years, the Mi'kmaq had used the Annapolis River as a travel route. The location of Paradise today was known to them as Nisoqe'katik, sometimes translated as "place of eel weirs." This was a traditional encampment site where Nova Scotia's Indigenous inhabitants caught an important part of their diet by constructing stone weirs that directed the eels into woven traps. Their food supply also came from hunting in the surrounding forest.

Lalanne's Paradis Terrestre was the farthest point on the river to be reached in the early wave of Acadian migration from Port Royal. It is identified by a census taken in 1687–88 as le Bout du Monde ("the end of the world"), the last village up the river. Only one couple was living there at that time, with their son and three daughters. They kept cattle and sheep, and had reclaimed four acres of marshland for cultivation, as well as farming an acre and a half of upland. French engineer Jean Delabat's 1710 map of the river settlements does not name Paradise, but shows on the south side of the river the homestead of Pierre DuPuis, who had moved upriver from Port Royal before 1678.

The Acadians who lived along the Annapolis River raised large, healthy families, which expanded the population of Paradise. The Mi'kmaq, who had become their firm allies, warned some of the residents of the impending deportation in 1755. Consequently, some Acadians were able to flee to the woods, where they were further helped by their Indigenous friends to evade the British and escape to safety in French territory. The less fortunate were carried away mostly to destinations in British colonies to the south.

After the deportation, the British destroyed the Acadians' homes, and their farms were left uncultivated. In 1759, Governor Charles Lawrence invited New Englanders to come and take the Acadians' place to provide food for the colony. When these settlers began to arrive in the 1760s, townships were created along the river to receive them.

Paradise and West Paradise across the river were originally part of the township of Wilmot, which was granted in 1764 to a group of settlers known as Planters, mostly from Massachusetts. And so they came sailing up the Annapolis River as their Acadian predecessors had done, until they arrived at Paradise. The extensive settlement consisted of twelve 500-acre land grants. The newcomers revived the deserted farms and extended them by clearing more upland. As they built their homes and planted orchards, tradition has it that they found the cellars of Acadian houses.

The Planters were joined in the 1780s by Loyalist families. The early years were difficult, as the settlers dealt with droughts, pests, and poor harvests, but Paradise slowly grew to become the major village in the township. William Inglis Morse, a descendant of one of the Loyalist families, summarizes the development of the community from the 1760s onward in his book titled *Local History Of Paradise, Annapolis County, Nova Scotia, 1684–1936*: "Aside from farming, the principal occupation, a few minor industries arose in the course of time, the building of five or six small ships, the erection of sawmills, one or two gristmills, tanneries, a small beaver hat shop, a window and sash factory, one carriage shop and the cheese factory."

Among these early entrepreneurs were shipbuilders Nathaniel Parker, Stillman Bent, and William Saunders. In about 1780, Jonathan Leonard built a flour mill on Leonards Brook and another on Starratt Brook. They were operated by his descendants for two or three generations. In 1817, Lieutenant-Governor George Ramsay, Lord Dalhousie, visited the area and reported in his journal that he stayed at "Mr. Lennard's, a miserable house, but most civil and obliging family." Samuel Morse ran a gristmill, which remained in his family for many years, while Charles Covert and his sons ran what W. I. Morse describes as "the most important tannery," but he does not mention others. Seth Leonard kept an inn, where it was said the Duke of Kent stayed in the late 1700s when travelling to Annapolis Royal along the newly established Post road from Halifax. Joseph Roland manufactured hats from beaver fur, of the style that had been fashionable in France in the seventeenth century and was still popular among the Acadians. The price was five dollars.

By the nineteenth century, Paradise was a busy place. As the roads improved, the market for wheeled vehicles grew among the general population, and William Henry Bishop opened his carriage factory in the community in 1857. Stagecoaches brought the mail, which residents picked up at what was known as a way office. Communications improved again after 1870, with the coming of the railway; businesses flourished, and a regular post office was opened. By the middle of the 1870s, there were about four hundred residents including merchants, a cooper, and a blacksmith. There was a shoemaker, and what W. I. Morse describes as "a sort of peripatetic furniture maker." For some time, two men named Barbour and Batten operated a cheese factory in Paradise, using milk from local dairy farms. The factory appears on a map of Annapolis County made by Ambrose Church in 1876, but it closed in about 1885. Sawmills continued to operate in the 1880s, and lumber was shipped downriver for export from Bridgetown.

Education was valued by the settlers, who considered literacy essential to people's ability to understand the Bible. Settlement was challenging in early days and the first schools were operated in private homes until a schoolhouse was built. Even then, stories circulated about the first teacher in the community, who was often drunk. A new school replaced the first one in 1831, with a teacher named Asaph Marshall, known as "Uncle Asaph," who taught until 1838 and raised the standard of education in Paradise. Good teachers continued to be hired, and in 1850 the Paradise school was recognized for its excellence by the provincial superintendent of education. A new single-room public schoolhouse was built in the mid-1860s, after the passing of the Free School Act, with an addition in about 1880. In 1894, the Paradise Academy was opened in a new building that still stands. With a declining population, it closed in 1979, and has since served various community purposes.

Anglicans in the area belonged to the parish of Wilmot, where a parish church was built in 1787, but most of the population of Paradise belonged to the Baptist Church, which opened in 1810. A new building replacing the original one was completed in 1882 and is still standing. The Evergreen Baptist Church in West Paradise was built in the late 1850s and originally served as

Cutting hay in Paradise before the Second World War. Acadians cut hay here in the seventeenth century. The church and river are in the distance.

a meeting house where worship services, town meetings, singing classes, and other community gatherings took place. It was also used as a schoolhouse from about 1860 until 1887, when it was dedicated for sole use as a church.

In the early twentieth century, Paradise was still primarily an agricultural community, and the apple industry was flourishing. Barrels of apples destined for exportation left from the Paradise railway station, and there was a ready market for farm produce. But change was coming. After the Second World War, the demand for apples dropped off, and many family farms ceased to operate. Young people moved away for higher education and found employment in larger centres.

The community has had some interesting residents. Some Mi'kmaq continued to live in the Paradise area for many years. The last of these was Heggie Lukie, who was born in 1834. He made his living as a guide, operating in various places in North America. He returned to live in Paradise where he died in 1941 at the age of 108.

A distinguished native of Paradise, writer and historian William Inglis Morse, quoted above, was born in 1874 to an old established Loyalist family. After graduating from Acadia University, he moved to the United States, was ordained in the Episcopal Church, and served for twenty-five years in the ministry. His passion was historical research, and he amassed an important collection of historical documents, which he donated to Acadia, Dalhousie, and other universities. He maintained a keen interest in his native province until his death in 1952.

In 1942, the Paradise general store acquired an unusual tenant. Otto Strasser, a German politician who had been expelled from the Nazi Party in the 1930s because of his opposition to Hitler, fled from Germany when Hitler came to power. Strasser spent ten years of his exile as a resident of Paradise.

Today, there are still farms in Paradise where the Acadians once grew crops. Some residents are self-employed and work from home, and others find the community a satisfying place for retirement. The recently formed Paradise Historical Society is dedicated to keeping the community's history alive by establishing a museum in the former Paradise Academy building, maintaining the village's Heritage Garden, and organizing workshops. A sign at the entrance to the village reads "Welcome to Paradise."

Upper Falmouth

The area known to the Mi'kmaq as Pesikitk lies at the lower end of the river we now call the Avon. The Mi'kmaw name for the river is Tuitnuk, and it was one of the traditional travel routes between the interior and the Minas Basin for thousands of years. The Mi'kmaq established campsites along the river, where they fished, hunted in the nearby forests, and as time went on, began to cultivate a few crops.

In the late 1600s, several Acadian families came to the area and established small farming villages along the marshy banks of what is now the Avon River. Like other rivers flowing into the Minas Basin, it is tidal for some distance, and there were extensive salt marshes on both sides that often flooded at high tide. The Acadians constructed dykes, drained the marshland, and built their homes on the higher ground overlooking their fields. The parish of Sainte-Famille was established on the west side of the river in 1698. The Acadians called the estuary area Pisiquid (spellings vary), after the Mi'kmaw name, and gave the same name to the lower reaches of the river, while they called the upper part rivière de l'Ascension.

This is where Germain Landry and his family were working six arpents (just over two hectares) of land, while their neighbours—Pierre, Michel, and Jean Forest—operated the next farms downstream. Most of them owned between ten and fifteen cattle and as many as seventeen sheep, while some also raised a few pigs. Their farms were productive and their families healthy. Germain Landry had three sons, Germain, Abraham, and Pierre; Pierre established a farm in what is now the Upper Falmouth area, while his brothers worked the dyke lands across the rivière de l'Ascension. By 1707, Pierre was married with a young son and was raising cattle, sheep, and hogs.

Seven years later, Pierre's family had increased, with two more boys and two girls. He and his neighbours pastured their livestock, cut hay, and grew some crops on the reclaimed marshlands; they built their homes, planted their orchards, and cultivated their gardens on the upland above the river. The dyke lands at Upper Falmouth, visible today from the Falmouth Dyke Road, date back to the days when the Landrys and their Acadian neighbours drained the marshes beside the Avon River. Their descendants continued to pasture their livestock, cut their hay, and harvest their crops until the fall of 1755, when British soldiers came to round them up and march them to Grand Pré to be deported with their compatriots. The land is still partially under cultivation today.

In the 1760s, the British authorities were anxious to redistribute the Acadian farmlands to settlers who would revive them and grow food for not only themselves but also for Halifax residents. The parish of Sainte-Famille became the township of Falmouth and home to immigrants from New England, where land was becoming scarce. The Planters, as they were known, were happy to come to a place where they found good farmland waiting for them. Falmouth town grew up across the river from Windsor, and the farmlands at Upper Falmouth were brought back into production. The dykes were repaired with the help of Acadians who had escaped deportation or who had been allowed to return in 1764, after the end of the Seven Years War. The new settlers expanded their farms farther onto the uplands to the west, which proved fertile and productive. At the end of the American Revolution, they were joined by Loyalist refugees. St. George's Anglican Church was built at Upper Falmouth in 1786.

In about 1763, Joseph Frederick Wallet DesBarres, a Huguenot from Montbéliard, acquired a large tract of land once worked by Pierre Landry, near the junction of the West Branch with the main Avon River. There he operated a farm and built a manor house that he called Castle Frederick on his five thousand–acre estate. It was a large establishment: by 1770, the staff consisted of forty-one men and thirteen women, as well as boys and girls, and included some Acadians who had evaded deportation. In 1765, DesBarres built an observatory near the house, which he initially used to check the accuracy of his surveying instruments. A few years later, he bought some of the best astronomical instruments available for his observatory, which was among the first to be established in North America.

At about this time, DesBarres began working on the series of coastal surveys that he later incorporated into an atlas published with the title *The Atlantic Neptune*. He employed several young naval officers as assistants in his drawing offices. The charts were considered the most useful and accurate representation of the coast of northeastern North America at that time. DesBarres's surveys took him away from home for months at a time each summer, and during his absences he turned over the management of the property to his mistress, Mary Cannon, with whom he had six children. During the winters at Castle Frederick, he worked on the preparation of the charts.

DesBarres did not spend much time in Castle Frederick once this part of his work was completed. By 1774 he was in England, where he compiled *The Atlantic Neptune* and saw it through to its publication in 1777. He remained an absentee landlord for much of his life: he spent several years in England, claiming compensation for expenses incurred during the production of the atlas, including the cost of the observatory. Here he met Martha Williams, with whom he would have eleven children. In 1784, he was appointed lieutenant-governor of the newly established colony of Cape Breton. He remained there until 1787, after which he lived in England before serving as lieutenant-governor of Prince Edward Island. He died in Halifax in 1824 at the age of 102. He seems never to have returned to live permanently at Castle Frederick, nor to Mary Cannon, who continued to manage the estate and DesBarre's other properties

DesBarre's Castle Frederick; the building to the left is probably his observatory.

for many years. In his absence, she was reputed to have taken up with an Irish labourer on the estate, and meanwhile she raised their children. A few years before his death, DesBarres transferred the Castle Frederick estate, which had been allowed to deteriorate during his long absence, to his four surviving children. It has been rejuvenated by his descendants.

The Avon River widens just below Castle Frederick, and this was for many years the lowest point where a bridge could be built. In the early nineteenth century, the main road from Halifax to Annapolis Royal crossed the river here. A map made in 1800 shows "The Road from Three Miles Plain near Windsor in Hants County to the New Bridge on the River Avon & thence to Bishops Bridge on the Gaspereau River." The newly constructed road ran in a direct line from Upper Falmouth to Horton, regardless of the steep hills noted by travellers such as Lord Dalhousie who describes it in *The Dalhousie Journals* as a "beautiful though very hilly road." For many years, as this was the only bridge across the Avon, Upper Falmouth became a busy place. Stagecoaches used the bridge, and a cluster of houses grew up at the crossroads. In 1836, the bridge was superseded by a covered bridge at Windsor, which carried the main road on its new route through Falmouth, bypassing Upper Falmouth. The "beautiful though very hilly road" now only partially exists.

Today, a modern bridge crosses the Avon below Castle Frederick. A road leads up from the bridge past the Anglican church to an intersection at Upper Falmouth. The road to the left leads to Castle Frederick, and the road to the right runs through Upper Falmouth along the river, past the dyke lands that are still farmed today. On the upland slopes are a vineyard and winery, Sainte-Famille Wines, whose name recalls the former Acadian parish. DesBarres's descendants, the Bremner family, continue to work the farm at Castle Frederick, where they have generously opened trails to the public. Archaeologists have found evidence there of the earlier Acadian occupation of this land, as well as the remains of the manor house. This is a place steeped in history.

Albert Bridge

You may have heard the song "Out on the Mira," celebrating the beautiful river in eastern Cape Breton that runs northeastward to the Gulf of St. Lawrence. For much of the Mira's length it consists of a series of lakes, some of which are a good kilometre wide. They were formed by glacial deposits left at intervals along the river valley after the last Ice Age, damming back the current. In these places the river narrows, allowing crossing points where today there are bridges. The song mentions Marion Bridge, but the largest of the Mira communities, and the most easily accessible, is Albert Bridge.

Albert Bridge—such a Victorian sounding name! However, the village is not, as people might think, named after the late Prince Consort but after the son of the man responsible for the bridge's construction, and its history goes back much farther than the nineteenth century. Like other major rivers in Nova Scotia, the Mira once served as a travel route for the Mi'kmaq between their seasonal camps in the forests along the river and the coast. They called the river Sookakade, "the silver place."

The earliest European inhabitants on the Mira were the French, who came from Louisbourg in the first half of the eighteenth century to clear land for farming. The fertile banks of the lower reaches of the river are not far from the fortress, and during the French regime in Île Royale, a small community was established in the area around today's Albert Bridge. A ferry crossed between the farms that were established on both sides of the river that they called the Miré. It is said to have been named in 1746 after a French officer, though other sources claim it had been named by Portuguese fishermen long before, after a place in their home country.

The rocky soil immediately around Louisbourg was not suitable for agriculture, so the farms on the banks of the Miré were an essential source of food for the fortress. The most important of these farms, *la Ferme de l'Hospital*, was operated on behalf of the Brothers of Charity, who had a large concession south of the river. The brothers were in charge of the hospital at Louisbourg, and fresh meat and vegetables from the farm supported the hospital and its patients. Fifty cords of wood were also brought to the fortress each year.

Several other individuals were granted land along the river, including soldiers from the fortress who were prepared to operate farms to supply the garrison. The most successful of these farms was owned by Mathurin Le Faucheux *dit* Longevin, who received a concession in 1734 on the north side of the river at what is now Albert Bridge. He raised oats, buckwheat, peas, and beans and harvested hay for his cattle.

As early as 1727, the French had established a brickyard on the south side of the river, a short distance downstream, where the Mira River Provincial Park is today. Here, clay suitable for brick-making can be found along the riverbank. Both the farm produce and the bricks used for construction at the fortress were sent by ship to Louisbourg.

After the final British defeat of the French, Île Royale was renamed Cape Breton Island, and the Miré became first the Miray and later the Mira. The British did not immediately take formal steps to replace the French population; they were chiefly interested in identifying the island's mineral resources. In fact, an order forbidding the granting of land in Cape Breton was issued in 1763 and rescinded only in 1784, when Loyalists were brought to the island. Other immigrants took advantage of the opportunity, and most of the original settlers on the Mira were Gaelic-speaking Scots who had lost their homes at the time of the Clearances.

Sydney was the main centre of population on the island, and a rough road linked the town with the fishing village of Louisbourg, where some Loyalists had settled. The road came to the river at the spot where the waterway narrows and that is now Albert Bridge. A 1794 map marks the "King's Ferry" where travellers crossed. In the early 1800s, a group of Scots settled there on land formerly cultivated by the French. Among the original families were Burkes, MacKinnons, MacDonalds, McCaulays, McVicars, and McMillans. Some of their descendants still live in the area. The language of the community was Gaelic, and this remained the common language for several generations.

A ferry continued to link the two sides of the river, and the community soon became known as Mira Ferry. For many years, this remained the name of the village that grew up on both sides of the river. The residents made their living mostly by farming and logging. A new brickyard replaced the former French operation at the site now known as Brickyard Road. It continued to operate until 1922.

Because of its central position between Sydney and Louisbourg, Albert Bridge became the major community in the surrounding region. Here churches, schools, and other services became centred over the years. The Union Presbyterian Church was opened 1857 to replace three smaller churches at Port Morien, Marion Bridge, and Catalone. The first services were in Gaelic, which was the language of most settlers in the area. Planning for this church had begun in 1849, when land on the south side of the river overlooking the ferry crossing was purchased by Rev. Hugh MacLeod on behalf of the congregation. Construction began the following year. Each able-bodied parishioner was required to contribute three weeks' labour to the building of what came to be known simply as the Ferry Church, although by the time it opened, the ferry had been replaced by a bridge. The church, which can seat a thousand people, is still standing. It has retained many of its original features, including its pulpit, box pews, gallery, and precentor's box. In 2009, it was designated one of Canada's Historic Places.

The majority of the population of Albert Bridge was Presbyterian, but there were a few Roman Catholics in the community, and in 1877, a small Roman Catholic church, St. Joseph's, was built on the south side of the river. It was enlarged in the 1870s to accommodate a larger congregation of up to two hundred people.

In 1849, as traffic on the road increased, a bridge was installed to replace the ferry. It was named after Albert Munro, whose father, William Henry Munro, represented Nova Scotia in the British Parliament and had pressed for its construction. The former community of Mira Ferry now became known as Albert Bridge. The structure was a swing bridge, which could be opened to allow traffic to pass up and down the river. There are no falls on the Mira below Victoria Bridge, near the head of the river, and before today's roads were built, transportation of goods and passengers between the communities all along the river was largely by water, with scows carrying supplies for the village stores. By the late 1800s, steamers were plying the waters of the Mira, and when the railway was built, Lou Petrie ran a steamboat service upriver from the train station at Mira Gut. By the end of the century, communities along the river were also connected by locally owned telephone services.

In the nineteenth century, and well into the twentieth, every small community had its one-room school, and children walked to school as a matter of course. In the 1950s, the Union School was opened at Albert Bridge to replace smaller schools in surrounding communities. The Albert Bridge School was closed in 2000 and replaced in turn by the Riverside School, which now serves students from the area up to grade eight.

In the days of horse-drawn traffic, Albert Bridge was a convenient stopping place between Sydney and the fishing community of Louisbourg. In the early 1900s, William Burke's hotel offered rest and refreshment for travellers. Today, the community remains a tourist centre with services, accommodation, and a campground, and offers services to summer residents in cottages on the river. In 1965, the Province of Nova Scotia bought the former brickyard land for a provincial park.

The Union Presbyterian Church at Albert Bridge was built in 1857 by members of the congregation and is still in use.

The original bridge was replaced by a stronger structure, and the present bridge was built in 1970. It is busy in summer, carrying tourist traffic on Trunk 22 between Sydney and Louisbourg. Travellers who pause at Albert Bridge can visit its historic Union Presbyterian Church, which is host to Gaelic concerts during the annual Celtic Colours Festival. Visitors may also enjoy a visit to the Mira River Provincial Park on Brickyard Road, with a wide range of outdoor activities on the site where bricks were once made for buildings in Fortress Louisbourg.

2

BUILDING THE
NOVA SCOTIAN MOSAIC

Nova Scotians can count a variety of ethnic or cultural groups among their communities' founders and current-day residents. The Mi'kmaq remain a significant segment of today's population. Early on, German, French, and Swiss Protestants were brought to Nova Scotia to create a balance with the Catholic Acadian population and were provided with land in and around Lunenburg. After the Acadians were deported, they were supplanted by people from New England where land was becoming hard to find. These newcomers were eager to take up the offer of formerly Acadian farmland.

Many inland communities have associations with specific groups of people who, for various reasons, came to make their homes there, and where their descendants may still be found. Highland Scots formed the majority of British settlers in the late eighteenth and early nineteenth centuries, when hundreds of them were evicted from their homes by their landlords who preferred to use the land to pasture the more profitable sheep. Many of them sought the mountains of Cape Breton or the undeveloped land of northern Nova Scotia.

After the American Revolution, Loyalists from different regions of the United States who wished to remain under British rule came to the new townships of Shelburne and Digby, from which some of them spread inland or joined their compatriots in Planter townships. Among them were former slaves who had fought for the British and were offered land and their freedom. More Blacks came with the returning troops after the War of 1812. Black communities were laid out in inland areas like Preston and Hammonds Plains.

The mid-nineteenth century saw a wave of Irish immigrants. Driven by poverty that was exacerbated by the great potato famine, they arrived to seek a better life in Nova Scotia. They frequently ended up, like the Scots, in Cape Breton and northern Nova Scotia. As the nineteenth century progressed and industries began to develop, both skilled workers and labourers were recruited from Britain and continental European countries to operate mines and factories in many parts of the province. In the twentieth century, two world wars brought refugees and war brides. In the aftermath of war, professional immigrants seeking to escape devastation and austerity added to the multicultural population we know today.

FOREIGN PROTESTANT FAMILIES

When Britain first gained permanent control of Nova Scotia, the population consisted of their garrison at Fort Anne, the Acadian farmers, and the well-established Mi'kmaq. When Halifax was founded in 1749, Britain and France were still competing for control of the rest of North America. The presence of so many French-speaking Roman Catholic Acadians worried the British authorities, who decided that more Protestant settlers were needed. English citizens were reluctant to emigrate, so to recruit settlers for Nova Scotia agents were sent to the German Palatinate, the Montbéliard region of southeastern France, and parts of Switzerland, where Lutherans and Calvinists were a minority and subjected to discrimination. Shiploads of so-called Foreign Protestants began to arrive in 1750; they were mostly settled in Lunenburg on grants of town lots and also farm lots, where inland communities like Blockhouse grew up. Later generations moved farther inland and discovered fertile terrain in the New Germany area.

Blockhouse

What is a blockhouse? It's a rudimentary military defensive structure, a small fort built of heavy timbers, intended to protect communities against enemy attack. Typically, it consists of two storeys, with an overhanging upper storey to allow the defending soldiers or militiamen to fire down on attackers. A number of them were constructed in Nova Scotia during the second half of the eighteenth century; the only surviving example is Fort Edward, in Windsor. Some were built in Lunenburg County, and there the name Blockhouse persists in what is now a small community at the intersection of Routes 3 and 324, the former site of one of these structures.

Blockhouse lies inland from Mahone Bay. When Lunenburg was established in 1753, families were granted farm lots outside the town to provide food for the community. A series of thirty-acre farm lots known as the Northwest Range was laid out on the fertile drumlins between Lunenburg and what is now the town of Mahone Bay, which was at that time called by its Mi'kmaw name, Mushamush. Many of the Northwest Range farm lots were initially granted to French-speaking families from Montbéliard.

Life was difficult in the early days of the settlement. Lunenburg had been established in the Mi'kmaw territory of E'se'katik. Acadian settlers had joined the Mi'kmaq there and called their community Merligueche, from its Mi'kmaw name. The two groups lived peaceably together and were allied against the British in the struggles to control Nova Scotia. When the Acadians were dispossessed and Merligueche was replaced by the town of Lunenburg, the Mi'kmaq continued to resist British occupation of their territory. After a Mi'kmaw raid on Lunenburg in 1756, the government ordered the construction of blockhouses to defend both the town and farm lots. One of these was to be on the Northwest Range.

This blockhouse was built in 1756 by a local landowner, Captain Ephraim Cook. He brought the building materials from Halifax in a sloop provided by the government, which also sent a party of Rangers to man the fort. It was one of three to be constructed that year to protect the approaches to the town of Lunenburg and the outlying farming areas. The fort was strategically placed on a hill above Mushamush and was linked by road to the other blockhouses, one in Mushamush and one on the LaHave River.

Mather Byles DesBrisay, in his *History of the County of Lunenburg*, tells us that the commanding officer had instructions to send out detachments to patrol the area near the farmsteads, where they were also to sleep at night to ensure the safety of the inhabitants. He might send reconnaissance parties farther afield, at his discretion, making sure there was always an adequate number of men left to guard the blockhouse. Supplies were to be closely monitored and used only when strictly necessary. The order read: "Great care must be taken of the ammunition and utensils in the blockhouse....Upon any alarm, or appearance of an enemy, you are to send notice thereof to your commanding officer; and in the meantime you are to act with the utmost vigor in attacking the enemy, defending your own position, or sending reinforcements to any other party that may be attacked."

In spite of these precautions, in March 1758 raiders attacked the Northwest Range, killing all four members of the Ochs family and one other woman, a Mrs. Röder. The number of Mi'kmaw casualties is not recorded. In September of that same year, raiders attacked a household in Mushamush, killing three people, and a detachment of militiamen was dispatched to seek them out, without success. Also, a ten-year-old boy was abducted on his way home from an errand. But by the end of 1759 the raids had stopped, and the following year a Peace and Friendship Treaty was signed by Governor Charles Lawrence and Chief Paul Laurent of the Mi'kmaq in the LaHave area.

Although the farming families of the Northwest Range no longer feared raids, they lacked the amenities available in the town of Lunenburg, where churches, schools, and other services were being established. A Montbéliard man by the name of George Frederick Bailly was appointed by the Society for the Propagation of the Gospel in Foreign Parts (SPG), an English missionary organization, to run a school in the town for the French-speaking children of his compatriots. Initially, it was successful, but when most of those families moved to live on their farm lots, the number of attendees dwindled. The Northwest Range, where many of the Montbéliard families had settled, was too far away for the children to walk to school every day, and families could not afford to board them in Lunenburg.

In about 1765, a project was launched to build a schoolhouse in the Northwest Range, where it was hoped that Mr. Bailly would teach during the winter months. From May to October, however, everybody, including quite

One of Lunenburg's old blockhouses, ca. 1800.

young children, had to work the farms; without the support, families could not survive. Even the schoolmaster had to work his patch of land. The schoolhouse was not built, some say because the settlers could not agree on a location. For a while one of the settlers gave instruction to the local children in his home, while Bailly visited occasionally to supplement his efforts.

In 1771, the Reverend Peter de la Roche was sent by the SPG to minister to Lunenburg's English and French inhabitants. He also promoted education for settlers' children, and attempted to establish a proper school for the Northwest Range families. A prosperous Swiss settler, Sebastian Zouberbuhler, donated money toward its construction. Bailly took over the teaching, but the population was already decreasing as many families had been lured away to become tenant farmers for J. F. W. DesBarres at Tatamagouche. The remaining settlers were unable or unwilling to provide adequate firewood and other supplies or to maintain the building. After three or four miserable winters, Bailly returned to Lunenburg where he taught a handful of students in his home.

The blockhouse was manned again during the American Revolution, when New England privateers frequently raided the area. In 1782, they attacked

Lunenburg and captured the militia leader, Colonel John Creighton. Although the threat now came from the sea rather than the land, and the worst damage was done in Lunenburg town, the residents of the Northwest Range would not sleep easily in their beds until peace was restored in 1783.

Lunenburg was again fortified during the War of 1812, and the militia was in readiness, but life on the Northwest Range farms continued largely undisturbed. More settlers came to the area in the nineteenth century, with lumbering and farming providing employment. As the population increased, clusters of houses grew up at Northwest, Fauxburg, and Blockhouse, which was the busiest of the three communities. By the 1880s, several sawmills had been established on brooks above the community, and a gristmill was operating. The centre of the settlement, with a schoolhouse, store, and blacksmith's shop, was situated at the intersection of the road between Lunenburg and Lake Mushamush and the post road from Halifax to Bridgewater and beyond. The track of the Nictaux & Atlantic Central Railway (later the Nova Scotia Central Railway) from Bridgewater to Mahone Bay and Lunenburg also crossed the post road here, and although there was no station, residents of small communities could usually catch a ride by flagging down the train. The Northwest Range blockhouse had been repaired and replaced a few times, but the final structure had become redundant when it burned down in 1874.

The community of Blockhouse saw a flurry of activity in 1896, when gold deposits were found nearby, but like other gold rushes, this one was short-lived as the resource was quickly exhausted. Exploration and mining in the area continued sporadically until just before the Second World War, although forestry and milling remained the community's primary industries. These, too, dropped off as the twentieth century progressed, bringing changes to Nova Scotia's economy.

Today, Blockhouse has a sawmill and lumberyard. It is home to a general store, an active volunteer fire department, and a variety of small businesses. Its independent Waldorf School has offered an alternative education encouraging creativity since 2001. A therapeutic riding centre provides programs for children with disabilities. The disused railway track through Blockhouse from Mahone Bay to Bridgewater has become the Adventure Trail, enjoyed by hikers and cyclists. Through changing times, this community remains alive and well.

New Germany

New Germany was described by Judge DesBrisay at the end of the nineteenth century in his *History of the County of Lunenburg* as "one of the most thriving agricultural districts of the county." It is still a commercial centre for the neighbouring farming country. It lies on the LaHave River, about twenty-eight kilometres above Bridgewater, just below New Germany Lake, which is formed by the widening of the river.

The LaHave was a well-used waterway for the Mi'kmaq, and the area that would become New Germany was home to several Indigenous families, including the Soulnow and Jeremy families, who had been living there for generations when white families first arrived. The pioneers were German-speaking members of Foreign Protestant families, and the community became known as New Germany because of the ancestry of many of its early residents. John Feindel came up the river from the family's farm lot in Upper LaHave with his wife Anna Barbara (Hebb) and their son John Adam in 1803 and settled at the foot of what would become known as New Germany Lake.

Their first home, as John Adam remembered, was "a trench or hole dug out of the side of a hill" covered with spruce boughs and birchbark. The floor was made of poles. This temporary accommodation would soon be replaced by a log cabin as the Feindels cut down trees to clear their land. In 1806, John and Anna's son John George was born, the first white child in New Germany. They went on to raise a large family. It was common for German families to give all their sons the first name John; they were generally known by their second name. John Feindel was given a licence of occupation for his land in 1811 on condition that he build a sawmill by the falls at the foot of the lake. His sons, (John) Adam, John, Jacob, George, and Michael, built houses on the family property, which was formally granted to them a few years later by Lord Dalhousie, who served as lieutenant-governor of Nova Scotia from 1816 to 1820.

William Woodworth arrived shortly after the Feindels. Woodworth's daughter was the first girl born in the community. Other pioneers were John Michael Varner, John Mailman, and Thomas Penny. DesBrisay tells us that Penny carried a bushel and a half of potatoes on his back up the rough trail along the LaHave River. The settlers would soon be growing their own potatoes. Some supplies still had to be brought in from outside, as John George

Feindel recalled: "My father and mother brought things out to the foot of Wentzells Lake, my mother walked along the shore with a tow rope."

A second contingent of settlers came from Annapolis and established themselves just south of the original group, at a spot known at that time as Chesley's Corner, after John Chesley, one of their number. The settlement became absorbed into New Germany, but the road from New Germany to Barss Corner is still known as Chesley Road. Another early settler was Nathaniel Morgan, who gave his name to the falls at the foot of the lake, where he built the first combined saw- and gristmill. Morgan's gristmill enabled the community members to have their grain processed close to home. Later, John Chesley also built a gristmill. These mills were the forerunners of several others that would bring prosperity to the area.

The settlers in New Germany soon established farms where the soil was arable. Unfortunately, some of these farms were situated on land that had been home to Mi'kmaw families for generations. In 1829, one of them, Joseph Soulnow, wrote a petition to the governor asking for land to replace the piece that he said his great-grandfather had owned "before anybody was in Nova Scotia" and that his grandfather had inherited. He reported that his family "had cleared on it, and planted appel trees, and fenced in a gardin, had a seller" and that a settler had taken the property from him. The result of the petition is not recorded, but it offers a striking example of the way the Mi'kmaq were displaced as white settlement expanded.

Toward the end of the nineteenth century, both John Adam and John George Feindel as old men described life in the early days of the isolated community. Before there was a gristmill, grain had to be carried by horseback to Kaulback's mill, over thirty kilometres away, as there was no road fit for a wagon. John Adam Feindel's mother, Anna, was known to visit Lunenburg alone on horseback, presumably to sell produce and pick up supplies. The Feindels raised cattle, sold butter in Lunenburg, and hunted and fished to supplement the produce of their farm. From an early age, their boys went hunting, set traps, and fished. They learned some of their skills, like "dipping" salmon with a net, from their Mi'kmaw neighbours. It was probably also from the Mi'kmaq that Anna Feindel learned to make "woods tea" from native plants, keeping "shop tea" in a trunk and bringing it out only when company came along.

The women of the community spun flax and wool for their clothing. A versatile craftsman, John Adam recalled that he wove homespun cloth on a hand loom, and even made shoes. He also told of stripping yellow birch with a jackknife and braiding the bark for a hat, which he sold.

As the century progressed, the plentiful supply of wood and the accessibility of water power made the processing of lumber a thriving industry in New Germany. Timber from the surrounding forest provided raw material for new mills in the town. Nathaniel Morgan's mill was replaced by a mill built by the Morgan Falls Pulp Company, which was established in 1893 by A. G. Jones and Sons and manager Joseph F. Hughes. At this time, paper made from wood pulp was replacing rag paper; there was a growing market for this product for newspapers and popular books. By 1895, fourteen cords of wood, mostly spruce, were used in the mill to produce over twenty tons of pulp per day. It was shipped by rail to Halifax for export to England in bales each weighing two hundred pounds.

The operation was later bought by the Acadia Pulp & Paper Mills Co. and managed by Joseph Feindel. It changed hands again in 1904, when it was purchased by members of the Davison family, who operated mills in Bridgewater. It became known as the LaHave Pulp Company, and for many years it was the largest employer in the town. In 1917, it was once more sold, this time to the American New Haven Pulp & Board Co., but retained its name. The LaHave Pulp Company continued to operate until 1958 and was the last pulp mill in the province still to be run by water power. The mill was replaced by a hydro-electric power plant.

Edward Zwicker built another mill that he operated with his sons, producing staves and shingles. The family, according to DesBrisay's *History of Lunenburg County*, abstained from alcohol, and "set a very good example of industry and close attention to business, which is widespreading and profitable." The mill continued to operate until the 1960s. The dam retaining the mill pond was later dynamited, but the mill stood until a few years ago. The road on which it stood is still known as Zwicker Mill Road.

Although milling, farming, and lumbering remained the community's principal occupations, other businesses grew up during the nineteenth century. The hat that John Adam Feindel had braided long ago was one of many that were made in New Germany, as the manufacture of straw hats became one of

Edward Zwicker's mill was turning out staves and shingles in the late nineteenth century, and operated until the 1960s. The building was later taken down.

the town's specialized industries. Whetstones were another product, manufactured by George McFadden at a nearby lake, and a tannery was established on the Barss Corner Road. In 1895, Otto Wile opened a cheese factory at New Germany, using milk from local farms.

Before a church was built, the Anglicans of New Germany attended services in Lunenburg, which meant walking to Upper LaHave on the Saturday, overnighting, and then proceeding to Lunenburg the next day. Sometimes "Parson Cochran" (the Reverend James Cochran, rector of St. John's, Lunenburg) would visit New Germany. His first service took place in John Feindel's barn, and he often held services by candlelight in the Woodworth kitchen. The Church of St. John in the Wilderness was built in 1844 and was consecrated by Bishop Inglis.

Not all the residents were of the Anglican faith. The first Baptist settler was Whitman Morton, who with some others came together to build a church in 1842. Fifty years later, Morton wrote a poem, quoted by DesBrisay in his *History of the County of Lunenburg*, in which this event is recalled:

They met in private dwelling house,
And there with prayer and song
The little church was organised
By Elder T. De Long

A third church was built by the Methodist residents of New Germany in 1850. It stood with its nearby parsonage on the Barss Corner Road. Trinity Lutheran Church was established by residents who were previously members of the nearest Lutheran congregation at West Northfield. The foundation stone was laid in 1904, and in 1948 a parsonage was built on an adjacent property.

Meanwhile, other services were established in the town. By the end of the nineteenth century, New Germany had stores, a school, a post office, and a hotel. The Nova Scotia Central Railway line between Middleton, Bridgewater, and Lunenburg opened in 1889, with a station in New Germany, enabling the local industries to ship their products by rail. The line became part of the Halifax and Southwestern Railway in 1902 and continued to serve New Germany as part of the Canadian National Railway until 1982. The train from Bridgewater was known as the Blueberry Express because it moved so slowly it was said you could hop off the front of the train and have time to pick some blueberries before rejoining the last car.

Today, the surrounding logging and farming operations ship their wood and agricultural products by truck. Christmas tree growing has become an important part of the rural economy. A range of small businesses serve residents and travellers. Students from the wider community attend New Germany Elementary School and New Germany Rural High School. The town is home to many services, including a seniors' club and a long-term care facility. New Germany remains a centre for the area's commercial and social activities.

PLANTERS AND LOYALISTS

The 1760s and 1780s saw two waves of immigrants to Nova Scotia from south of the border. The Planters from New England were descendants of early emigrants from Britain who, having escaped the constraints of the British social and religious establishment, had formed more democratic communities on their arrival in North America. These communities were regulated by town meetings instead of by the local laird or squire, and the settlers practised freedom of religion. When they took up the offer of land in Nova Scotia, they continued this way of life in the townships that were prepared for them. The Loyalists, who followed them after the American Revolution, may have preferred to live under British rule, but many of them found it difficult to adapt to life in Nova Scotia. While the Planters' task was to revive formerly cultivated farmland, the Loyalists often had to start from scratch, clearing their land, building shelters for themselves, and finding means to become self-sufficient. Some of them settled in established Planter communities. Other members of both groups either failed to take up their grants or moved on after a short time. Those who stayed formed solid communities.

Bridgetown

The Annapolis River runs through the valley of the same name, from the Caribou Bog to the Annapolis Basin. It was an important communication route for the Mi'kmaq, for Acadian farmers who came to the area, and later for British settlers. The Valley, as it is known, is the earliest inland area of Nova Scotia to be settled by Europeans, and one of the province's most productive farming areas.

In Port Royal, at the mouth of the Annapolis River, the Acadian population was increasing in the second half of the seventeenth century. Much of the land immediately around the town was already under cultivation. Moreover, the town was occasionally raided by New Englanders. Families in search of land that they could cultivate in peace began to advance up the Annapolis River, where they drained the marshland and established small communities. One of these grew up at what was once the head of navigation, in the place that we now call Bridgetown.

The Gaudets, whose ancestor Jean Gaudet and his family were among the earliest French settlers to come to Acadie in the 1630s, worked land on the Annapolis River, then known as the rivière du Dauphin, sometime in the later seventeenth century. Their settlement just east of today's Bridgetown was known as Gaudetville. Other Acadians settled in the area where the town now lies. Together the families dyked and drained the marshes, and lived and farmed here until 1755, when they were deported.

After Britain gained permanent control of Nova Scotia, the Mi'kmaq, who understandably resented the incursion into Indigenous territory, formed an alliance with some Acadians to conduct guerrilla warfare against the British. In 1711, fighting took place near the present-day Bridgetown between British soldiers and Indigenous forces from Castine. The British were travelling upriver when they were taken by surprise near Bloody Creek and suffered a humiliating defeat. The east side of Bloody Creek was the scene of a second confrontation in 1757, when Acadians who had escaped deportation attacked British soldiers as they marched upriver from Fort Anne. The British suffered many casualties and were forced to retreat. The locations of the two battles are now National Historic Sites, and a cairn at the second site commemorates the Battles of Bloody Creek.

In 1758 and 1759 respectively, Governor Lawrence issued proclamations inviting settlers from New England to come to Nova Scotia to work the farms that had lain abandoned since the Expulsion. In response to the governor's proclamation, a delegation of New Englanders arrived in Halifax in April 1759. After meeting with Lawrence and some of the council members, and agreeing to their terms, they were invited to view possible locations for their townships. They were escorted by Chief Surveyor Charles Morris to sites on the Bay of Fundy and the Annapolis River. Morris then proceeded to survey and lay out boundaries where the new townships would be established. Each had a town plot that would serve as an administrative centre and the site of the town meetings, which were the traditional form of local government among the New Englanders.

Granville Township, extending along the northern bank of the Annapolis River, was among the first to be established. The Granville town plot lay across the river from Annapolis Royal, but the township's farming communities expanded upriver as newcomers worked the former Acadian lands. Settlement extended to the former Gaudetville, the last place on the river that ships could reach from distant ports.

Among the New Englanders was a man named John Hicks, a Quaker from Rhode Island, who had been a member of a delegation that had come to Nova Scotia in April 1759 to discuss settlement terms. He organized a group of would-be settlers in the township of Falmouth. He had spent a few years there as a prominent community member before moving to land he had purchased in Granville Township, where farms had grown up on the north shore of the Annapolis River. Hicks settled on a bend of the river at the head of navigation, where a ford made it possible to wade across at low tide. He soon became one of the chief citizens of Granville Township, and he served as a member of the House of Assembly representing the township from 1758 to 1770.

Hicks did not remain in Granville Township for long afterwards. In 1772, he bought land on the south side of the river, in Annapolis Township, and moved across. He established a ferry, replacing the ford that formerly connected the two townships. As a result, the community became known as Hicks's Ferry. The name outlived him: he died in 1790, but his descendants remained in the area and became prosperous.

The area continued to be called Hicks's Ferry for many years, even after the construction of the first bridge over the river in 1805, which Lord Dalhousie described on a visit in 1817 as "a good wooden bridge." It lasted until 1878, when it was replaced by a covered bridge with a sign admonishing users to "keep to the left & walk your horses or you will be fined." In 1907, this bridge was replaced by a steel structure, and two others have since spanned the river in their turn. The area on the north side of the river remained a cluster of farms spread along its banks, with land reaching back over the North Mountain toward the Bay of Fundy.

It was not until 1821 that a resident of the township, Captain John Crosskill, oversaw the development of a town on the north bank. He laid it out in an orderly fashion by dividing the land into equal sized lots ninety feet square in a grid pattern. A few years later, the town's residents decided to rename the community Bridgetown. It would become the agricultural and industrial centre for the surrounding area.

By the end of the nineteenth century, Bridgetown had become a busy industrial community. The nearby forests provided a valuable resource; lumbering

Covered bridge at Bridgetown, with the warning: "Keep to the left & walk your horses or you will be fined."

and wooden shipbuilding were the first industries to be established. Joseph Howe visited Bridgetown in September 1828 and described the village in his *Western and Eastern Rambles* as "surrounded on all sides by cultivated country." Howe noted, "It is also a seaport where vessels of very heavy tonnage may come up the river." He also observed that the shipyards had produced several very fine vessels.

The demand for timber that had flourished during the Napoleonic Wars declined afterwards, but trading schooners still sailed away with loads of lumber and agricultural produce for export. Vessels sailed in on the tide, bringing goods from Boston and as far away as the West Indies to stock the stores of prosperous merchants. Soon, other industries developed, including a tannery, a bottling plant, and a cider plant.

The abundant supply of lumber spurred the growth of Bridgetown's furniture industry. John Bath Reed opened his factory around 1858, making bedroom and parlour furniture, and employing ten or more workers. Over the years, the operation became increasingly mechanized, and by 1878 the plant was known as J. B. Reed's Steam Cabinet Factory. It specialized in the production of "Jenny Lind" style chairs, named for the famous opera singer. Reed also established an organ factory, making both church and parlour instruments. The factory later offered a range of products from school desks to clothes dryers.

The Reed furniture factory was bought in 1895 by the firm of Curry Bros. and Bent, who advertised themselves as contractors and builders. They also offered a diverse range of products from their sash, door, and planing works: school, church, and office furniture, wood mantels, and miscellaneous building materials. Similar products were advertised at about the same time by John H. Hicks of Bridgetown. His firm also operated a sawmill, and the business remained in the Hicks family until after the Second World War.

Apples have always been a major crop of the Annapolis Valley, and in the early twentieth century, Minard Wentworth Graves set up a company in Bridgetown to manufacture cider vinegar from the abundant supply of second-grade fruit. The success of this enterprise made M. W. Graves and Company a major employer in the town. Graves later extended operations to produce dried apples. The business continued to expand after his death as his sons added canned fruit and juice among other products. The company is still operating but has since moved away from Bridgetown. For some years in the twentieth century, Larry McGuiness's Acadian Distillery was a major business in the town, producing Canadian whiskies, but that has now closed.

Bridgetown's most famous son was a descendant of John Hicks. Henry Davies Hicks is remembered as a lawyer, politician, leader of Nova Scotia's Liberal party, and one-time premier of Nova Scotia. He subsequently became dean of arts, vice-president, and finally president of Dalhousie University. He also served as a Canadian senator.

Bridgetown's industrial era came to an end in the first half of the twentieth century as technologies evolved and factories closed. The community's importance as a port, already losing ground to road and rail transportation, ceased completely in the early 1960s, when a causeway was built across the mouth of the Annapolis River, cutting the town off from the sea.

For many years, the post road from Halifax ran through Bridgetown, which was the last stop for stagecoaches before Annapolis Royal. It became Trunk 1 and remained the main route through the Valley for many years. Today, the town is bypassed by Highway 101. Its former industries have given way to a variety of small businesses. Bridgetown has changed from a bustling manufacturing town to a quiet, rural community with deep roots in the past.

Berwick

The town of Berwick lies just south of the Cornwallis River, near its source in what is known as the Caribou Bog. This is the heart of the Annapolis Valley's apple-growing country, and Berwick is known today as the Apple Capital of Nova Scotia.

Long before the first house was built in Berwick, the Mi'kmaq knew the Caribou Bog as part of their travel route from the Annapolis Basin to the Minas Basin. The Cornwallis River, known to the Mi'kmaq as Jijuktu'kwejk, flows eastward from the bog, which is fifty metres above sea level and is also the source of the Annapolis River (Te'wapskik) flowing westward. The bog was formed when the ice that had covered the Maritime provinces retreated some ten thousand years ago, at the time when the Indigenous people first came to the area. They established a portage trail across the bog, connecting the headwaters of the two rivers that served as their highways.

When the Acadians spread out from Port Royal toward the end of the seventeenth century, they built their villages along the lower reaches of what they named rivière du Dauphin, now the Annapolis River, and around the Minas Basin. To travel between the two groups of villages, they followed the example of the Mi'kmaq, building a rough road through the Caribou Bog, from rivière du Dauphin to rivière Grand Habitant, which the British renamed the Cornwallis River. In the 1760s, Planter settlers from New England took over the Acadian farms on the rivers and the Minas Basin. Some Planter families received grants in the area that would become Berwick, but they did not immediately develop their land, which remained vacant until the second generation began to populate the area.

Benjamin Congdon was a member of this second generation. His family, originally from Rhode Island, arrived in Nova Scotia in the 1760s. In 1810, Congdon came to the area and proceeded to build himself a house south of the

Cornwallis River on the road between the Annapolis and Cornwallis communities. He was soon joined by his brother, Enoch, and the spot became known as Congdons Corner or Congdons Settlement. Other descendants of Planter families who came at about this time were those of Samuel, Asa, and Kerr Beckwith; Eleazar Woodworth; and David and Desiah Shaw. They were followed by others, mainly Loyalist families. In 1827, Deacon William Parker came to the community with his wife, Susan, and infant son. James Brydon, born in Scotland, came at about the same time with his wife, Mary Ann, and opened a woodworking shop. Their first child, Isaac, was born in 1831. Other early residents included James Chipman Morse; William Davison, the first doctor; his successor, Dr. H. C. Masters; and John Joseph van Buren.

By 1825, there were enough children in the community that the first school was built. It was a primitive structure, soon replaced by a second building that lasted until 1851, when a third one was constructed. Its classrooms for boys were on the main floor; the upper storey comprised a Temperance Hall, also used for general community purposes, and a girls' school. The third school was designed by David Parker, a versatile man who became a Baptist minister, school inspector, furniture manufacturer, and writer.

Many of the original Planter families were Baptists, and in 1828 a Baptist church was opened in Berwick. Its first minister was the Reverend E. M. Saunders, the father of Margaret Marshall Saunders, author of the classic children's book *Beautiful Joe*. The church was originally known as the Second Cornwallis Baptist Church, a name it would retain until 1890, when it became the Berwick Baptist Church. It served a wide rural area around the town.

The second half of the century started well, as the community began to settle into a period of quiet prosperity and adopted its permanent name. In its earlier years, the name had changed several times. After Congdons Corner, now applied only to the central intersection, it was known variously as Pleasant Valley, Curreys Corner, and Davisons Corner. At a meeting of the residents in 1851, it was decided to adopt the name Berwick, after the Scottish town of that name.

The Western Stage Coach Company began to operate a mail and passenger service between Halifax and Annapolis Royal in 1829. Berwick's location on the road established it as a stagecoach stop, where horses were changed, passengers boarded or disembarked, and mail and freight were loaded and unloaded.

Originally the coach ran only three days a week, but by 1855 the service was daily. In 1856, a postal way office was established, which soon became a regular post office.

Changes came with the establishment of the railway from Windsor to Annapolis. A station was built in 1869, and trains soon replaced the stage-coach as the primary carrier for passengers, freight, and mail. The post office was relocated to the station, where Edward C. Foster became both postmaster and stationmaster. The arrival of the railway allowed local farmers to send their produce to market by train. The town expanded southward as businesses grew up near the railway station. One day in 1885, there was a stir in the community when a train derailed, resulting in some casualties. It seems that a fence had come down on the Chipman farm, allowing a cow to stray onto the line, with serious consequences for the passengers—and presumably for the cow.

In the second half of the century, Berwick became established as a commercial centre for the local farmers who came into town with their wagons to ship their produce and to purchase supplies. A variety of businesses were operating by 1900. There were stores selling meat, groceries, clothing, hardware, flour, and feed, a smithy and a tinsmith's shop, a brickyard, a creamery, and manufacturers of boots and shoes, furniture, and carriages. There were hotels, a bank, and a newspaper office. The *Register* was founded in 1891 by John E. Woodworth, who was both editor and publisher until 1919, when the business was sold. After several changes of ownership, the newspaper survives as the *Kings County Advertiser* and *Register*.

New denominational churches came to the community. The Methodists established a church there in 1857. In 1872, the annual Berwick Camp Meetings originated on the property of Edward C. Foster, as occasions for evangelization and spiritual renewal, open to all. In 1875, a site was selected for an Anglican church. Christ Church was originally built in Grafton, but the structure was moved to the larger community of Berwick the following year. A chancel and vestry were added to the original building, and the finished church was consecrated by Bishop Binney in 1883, as part of the parish of Aylesford. The Baptists still formed the majority of residents, and a parsonage for the minister was built in 1899.

The third school was replaced in 1884 by one which served, with additions, until 1934. Like other schools of the time, it was heated by wood stoves in the classrooms. Water came from a pump. Toilet facilities were out in the yard.

Berwick Station and apple warehouses in the 1930s, with the train track running past fields and orchards.

Although this was mainly an agricultural area, other industries were developing. In the 1880s, Pineo and Clark's Berwick Iron Foundry and Machine Shop produced a variety of machine work, including water wheels. By the end of the century, the Berwick Steam Mills, established in 1887 by E. R. Davison and H. W. Clark, were turning out building supplies of all kinds.

The twentieth century brought continued growth to Berwick, which was incorporated in 1923. New businesses came to the town. In 1924, Arthur E. Bezanson opened the Berwick Bakery, which his sons continued to run. A spur line of the railway brought flour to the plant. The Larsen meat-packing plant was established in 1939, and was later taken over by Maple Leaf Foods. It continued to operate until 2010.

By the beginning of the century, the surrounding area had become an important apple-growing area, and much of the local economy was based on the export of apples to markets in Britain and Europe. Farmers brought barrels of fruit to warehouses alongside the railway station which were operated by dealers such S. B. Chute, known as the "Apple King of the Valley." From there, the fruit was sent to Halifax for shipping. In 1907, the Berwick Fruit co-operative was established by a group of local farmers who saw much of their profit going to shippers and warehouse operators. They established their own warehouse beside the railway, which burned in 1923 and was replaced by a larger brick building that was known as the largest fruit warehouse in the Maritimes. The company provided a boarding house for its workers and operated a cooperage making barrels for shipping the fruit. The business was maintained until 1981, when it closed because of high operating costs and declining sales.

Not all apples were exported. In 1931, A. W. Stepanski opened a processing plant producing apple juice. He had plans to operate a distillery but was unable to obtain permission to do so. The business failed and was taken over by the M. W. Graves Company as Berwick Fruit Products. With the outbreak of war in 1939, the British market for fresh fruit came to a standstill. That same year, the company had begun to produce canned apples and pears, applesauce, and juice. Much of this was for export, but the war brought a change of plans. Britain ceased to import canned fruit in 1940 but provided a ready market for dried apples and vegetables produced by the company's dehydrating equipment. After the war, the company resumed production of canned fruit and juice. The plant was sold in the 1960s and changed hands several times before closing in 2004.

The overseas market for apples did not recover after the war, and the surrounding farms maintained some orchards but diversified their crops. Businesses in Berwick are also more diversified, but the town is still known as the Apple Capital of Nova Scotia. The Apple Capital Museum, established in 1998 to preserve Berwick's rich history, welcomes visitors.

Kentville

Kentville, now the shiretown of Kings County, lies at Cornwallis River's head of tide, where the river could be forded at low tide. Both Mi'kmaq and Acadians made use of this natural crossing place. It became known to the Mi'kmaq who lived in that area as Pinokoek, meaning "at Pineau's place." We don't know who this particular Pineau was; however, the Pineau or Pineo families in Nova Scotia seem to have been of Huguenot ancestry and came to Nova Scotia by way of New England in the eighteenth century. There were several Pineo families in Kentville and in the surrounding area by the time the 1861 census was taken, and there are Pineos living there today. The Acadians called the Cornwallis River la rivière St-Antoine, rivière des Habitants, or rivière Grand Habitant, and they created productive farms by draining the salt marshes along its lower reaches. The area north of the river was the parish of St. Joseph des Mines, which extended to the North Mountain.

When Planter settlers came to the area after the Expulsion to work the abandoned Acadian farms, the former parish of St. Joseph became the township of Cornwallis; the river and the town that was laid out near Starrs Point took the same name. Farm and town lots were granted to New Englanders, not all of whom stayed. Those who did soon established good farms, both on the drained marshland and on cleared upland in what has remained an important agricultural area. Although a ferry linked Cornwallis town with Horton Township on the south side of the river, its residents still felt very isolated, and many of them began to move to more convenient locations farther upriver, closer to the spot where it could be crossed.

The township of Horton had been established south of the Minas Basin and the Cornwallis River. It included the Acadian village of Grand Pré and the town of Horton at the mouth of the Gaspereau River. Before a bridge was built at Port Williams, the most convenient place to cross the river to conduct business or visit friends in Cornwallis Township was Pinokoek, where instead of relying on a ferry, people could use the ford. Several roads in both townships led to this crossing place, and in the 1780s a community grew up where the road from the ford met the post road to Annapolis Royal. It was originally known as Hortons Corner. Small vessels brought merchandise upriver and carried away produce from the surrounding farms. In 1788, a Loyalist named Henry Magee opened the first store and operated a sawmill and gristmill. Other merchants followed.

Hortons Corner grew slowly at first. Early in the nineteenth century, its bad reputation as a place of heavy drinking and rowdy behaviour earned it the locally known moniker, "the Devil's half-acre." In 1819, Lord Dalhousie attended the cattle show there, where he was welcomed by members of the local agricultural society who were putting on this event for the first time. *The Dalhousie Journals* record his observation that it "was but poorly attended. One half of the neighbourhood never had heard of it, & the other believed it to be nothing more than a drinking frolic, & staid at home." The community regained a better reputation, and in 1826 it was renamed in honour of the Duke of Kent, who had been in command of the military in Nova Scotia at the end of the eighteenth century.

The stagecoach from Halifax along the Valley road made a regular overnight stop at Kentville, leaving early the following morning for Bridgetown. When Joseph Howe was travelling along the Valley in 1828, he stopped overnight at what he called, in his *Western and Eastern Rambles*, "the sweet little village of Kentville." He was received with warm hospitality at the Kentville Inn by Mrs. Fuller, "who will make you as comfortable as heart can wish." At that time, he recorded there were about thirty houses clustered around the crossroads from which the town's earlier name was derived.

Kentville evolved as the shiretown of King's County; its first courthouse was a wooden building constructed in 1829 that included a jail. Because of its location as a communications centre, Kentville became the market town for local farmers. The ford continued in use until a bridge was built in the 1870s. Transportation continued to improve, when in 1868 the town was chosen as the headquarters of the Windsor and Annapolis Railway. The population grew rapidly after the station and the company's head offices were opened in 1869. The railway quickly became one of the community's major employers, with a car shop and engine house. The station was also the telegraph office, where people kept in touch with families in distant places and news of the world arrived. Freight was shipped and received. Passenger trains brought visitors to town.

Apple-growing had developed in the surrounding area as a major export industry in the second half of the century. The popular fruit was now shipped for export by rail, and autumn was a busy time as farmers came into the station yard with their wagons and ox carts laden with barrels of the orchards' bounty. When they had completed the formalities with station officials, they might adjourn to the station's lunchroom or simply linger about, exchanging the latest news with their neighbours and enjoying their day in town. The iron locomotive would pull in, blowing its whistle and belching clouds of steam, and the barrels would be loaded into boxcars. When the cargo was fully loaded, the whistle would sound again, and the train would head for Halifax where most of the apples would be transferred to vessels bound for England. The station was enlarged in 1889 with the addition of a baggage room, and twice more in 1904 and 1920 respectively, with extensions at each end, so that in the middle of the twentieth century it was an impressive building, with a tower, dormer windows, and a canopy that ran its entire length.

Kentville was the administrative centre for the county. By 1870, the population included the High Sheriff of the county, a judge, and several lawyers. There were Episcopalian, Presbyterian, and Catholic churches, a hotel, merchants' stores, tradesmen's shops, and a school. The settlers included railway workers, various merchants, blacksmiths, saddlers and harness-makers, manganese miners and quarrymen, carpenters and painters, barristers, and civic officials. In 1888, John I. Lloyd established a foundry that by 1895 had become the Lloyd Manufacturing Company, producing machinery of all kinds for sawmills throughout the province. After a fire in 1900, the plant was quickly rebuilt and added gasoline engines to its products. In 1892, the Aberdeen Hotel, a striking wooden building, opened near the railway station to accommodate the increasing number of travellers in the area. The railway bought the hotel in 1919 and renamed it the Cornwallis Inn.

The twentieth century ushered in many changes to the town. The old courthouse was replaced in 1903 by the brick-built Kings County Courthouse, which is now home to the Kings County Museum. Tuberculosis was common in Nova Scotia, and in 1904 Kentville was chosen as the site for a provincial sanatorium. It continued to treat tuberculosis patients until 1971, when its services merged with the Blanchard Fraser Memorial Hospital. This, in its turn, was succeeded in 1992 by the Valley Regional Hospital. In 1930, the wooden Cornwallis Inn was replaced by the large brick structure that still stands in the centre of the town. With ninety rooms, a ballroom, and meeting facilities, it was modified in 1960 to include some apartments but operated as a hotel until 1976, when it was wholly converted into apartments. The Lloyd company changed hands and became the Burrell Foundry and Machine Works, which continued to operate until 1987.

The town was busy during World Wars One and Two as troops trained at nearby Camp Aldershot, and rail traffic was especially heavy. The apple industry

Kentville in horse and buggy days, ca. 1900. The large building on the right is Lyons Hotel, on the left is St. Paul's Presbyterian Church, which became St. Paul and St. Stephen United Church in 1925.

had lost its chief export market at the outbreak of the Second World War. When business slowed after 1945, the railway, a major employer in Kentville, suffered a decline. A contributing factor was that an increasing amount of freight was carried by road, and many more people drove cars. Passenger service on the railway terminated in 1990, and the station was demolished. Three years later, freight service also stopped, and the rail shops were closed. The historic roundhouse, the last surviving railway building, was demolished in 2007.

A happier story is that of the Kentville Research and Development Centre, operated since 1911 by the federal government to carry out research about agricultural technology. Scientists there have developed plant strains suited to the Atlantic soils and climate and support the work of farmers with research in methods of production, processing, and storage. Hidden in a ravine behind the buildings and picnic ground is the research station's nature trail that runs along a brook toward a waterfall.

Kentville's Apple Blossom Festival has been a major attraction since 1933, bringing visitors each spring to watch the parade and enjoy the blossoms in the orchards. A more recent tradition is the annual display of pumpkin people scattered throughout the town. Today, the former railway town is an enterprising community with a variety of businesses, including Gaspereau Press, renowned for fine books. Kentville has survived changing times by diversifying its economy, welcoming visitors, and taking pride in its history

Bear River

The picturesque village of Bear River, known today for its scenic location and community of artists and craftspeople, lies in a narrow valley at the tidehead of the river from which it takes its name. But visitors should not expect to encounter a bear as they explore the area. Although the village has been known by various names, its present name, as we shall see, does not refer to wildlife prowling in the forest.

The first inhabitants were the Mi'kmaq, who still live in the area and named the river L'sitkuk, which is said to mean "flowing between high rocks." In the early years of the seventeenth century, when Champlain and his companions were living at the Port Royal Habitation on the other side of the Annapolis Basin, the Mi'kmaq were still the river area's only inhabitants, as they had been for ten thousand years. They travelled by canoe, between their inland dwellings above the tidehead and the Annapolis Basin, hunting, fishing, and gathering molluscs.

The French at the Habitation knew of the river, and originally called it rivière St. Antoine, which is how it appears on Champlain's map of Port Royal. It later became known as rivière Imbert after a man named Simon Imbert, who anchored one of the Habitation's supply ships at the river's mouth to escape a severe storm. The British anglicized this name to Bear River. Both names appear on Jacques-Nicolas Bellin's 1744 map of Port Royal.

The Habitation was abandoned in 1607, when the settlers were recalled to France. Five years later, Jean de Biencourt de Poutrincourt returned to Acadie and re-established the Port Royal settlement. The apothecary Louis Hébert, who had previously accompanied Champlain, returned with this second expedition. He took an interest in the agricultural potential of the region, and tradition has it that he planted a vineyard on the eastern hillside above Bear River. Although the French may have been aware of the river's possibilities, they did not develop the area before raiders from New England destroyed the Habitation, prompting Poutrincourt and most of the settlers to return to France.

After the British gained control of Nova Scotia in 1713, they initially took little interest in Bear River. It had no strategic importance, and although the French had recognized its agricultural value, it was not immediately developed for farming. It was some time before its potential for lumbering was realized. Bear River came to the attention of authorities only after the American Revolution, when land was needed for Loyalist refugees and disbanded troops. In 1783, plots in the area were given to disbanded German soldiers of the Waldeck Regiment who had fought on the British side. English-speaking settlers joined them, and a community grew up where two branches of the river come together at the head of tide. The Loyalist cemetery records the names of many of the community's earliest residents.

Many of the original German grantees moved away from the area, but British settlers remained. Their earliest buildings were log cabins, and there was a great celebration after the completion of the first frame house. It was built by Captain O'Sullivan Sutherland on the eastern slope above the river. The housewarming party, according to *Historic Sketch of Bear River*, published in 1893 (author unknown), was a riotous affair to which "everybody who was entitled to be somebody was invited, and music, dancing and drinking made the hours roseate until the dawn of the next day." The settlers began their new lives by farming the fertile slopes above the river and soon developed industries in the valley. The surrounding forests provided both hardwood and softwood, so lumbering became a mainstay of the economy. In those early days, when mechanization was unknown, logs were hauled out of the forest by teams of horses or oxen or floated down the river. Water-driven sawmills were built along the brooks running down from the surrounding hills.

By the 1890s, the six lumber mills that operated in the area supplied material for the other major industry, which was shipbuilding. The wide tidal range of the Bay of Fundy makes the river deep and navigable at high tide, while the low tide exposes marshes and mud flats. Bear River's shipyards employed many residents of the small community. Locally built trading vessels left Bear River bound for England, Europe, and the West Indies with cargoes of lumber. They returned with goods with which merchants supplied the residents' needs, including household items, hardware, tea, sugar, molasses, and rum. Nineteenth-century wood products included barrels used to transport locally grown apples and other fruit. Some of the barrels manufactured in Bear River were sold to sugar refineries in Halifax and Moncton. Barrel staves were also exported, and a variety of other wooden items were produced by the local sawmills.

The major employers in Bear River were the brothers Wallace and Willard Clarke, whose company, Clarke Brothers, was established in 1877. They operated a sawmill at Lake Joli, from which lumber was dragged to the wharf by horses and oxen. It was shipped to overseas markets and to Ontario in their barquentine *Ethel Clarke*. They also had premises in the town, where their store sold dry goods, groceries, general merchandise, and insurance. In 1915, the mill became a hardwood operation, producing a range of items from door frames and window sashes to toy furniture and clothespins. In 1921, the firm opened a pulp mill beside the bridge at Bear River, but it was short-lived. The mill at Lake Joli burned in 1923.

The demise of the age of sail curtailed shipbuilding and reduced the demand for lumber; however, sawmills continued to operate in Bear River into the twentieth century. A stave mill operated until the 1950s, but demand for barrels was also declining. A steam mill was established by the Darres Brothers in 1942. A second one that followed burned down and was replaced by an electricity-powered mill. It was operated by Gerald Buckler until 1992, when the last lumber was sawn, and milling ceased in Bear River.

The river valley here is very narrow, defined by steep hills on either side, leading to the name Little Switzerland, by which the place is sometimes known. Because of the lack of land beside the meagre riverbanks, many of Bear River's buildings, particularly its warehouses and other commercial structures, either extended over the water on stilts or were built on reclaimed land protected from the tide by strong stone walls. A few buildings by the bridge are still standing on stilts. With the prosperity generated by the village's industries, some residents built fine houses that are still standing today on streets sloping toward the river.

An interesting feature of the community is that the river forms the boundary between Annapolis and Digby Counties; residents pay their taxes to two different authorities, depending on which side they live on. An attempt was made to give the two sides of the river different names: the Annapolis side was to be known as Bridgeport, and the Digby side as Hillsburg. Not surprisingly, this was met with indifference by most residents, and the compact little community retained its current name. Until the construction of the bridge that

Around 1900, Bear River was the scene of popular canoe races. Note the buildings on stilts in the background.

serves as part of Highway 101, Bear River's bridge at the head of tide was the lowest crossing point. Several roads from both sides of the river come together here, bringing traffic from all directions to the village.

Tourism began to develop in Bear River toward the end of the nineteenth century, when hunting and fishing attracted wealthy vacationers, and the Clarke brothers added outfitting and guiding to their enterprises. The Mi'kmaq who lived nearby had a reputation as skilled guides. In the second half of the twentieth century, many artists and craftspeople came to this remote community. Today, tourists come to Bear River to enjoy the scenery and visit the arts and crafts shops and studios that now occupy the former premises of nineteenth-century businessmen. The hospitality industry benefits from the village's attractions, which include the river itself. It is possible to sit on the deck of a local café or in the little park by the bridge and watch the tide turn.

We do not know how much truth there is in the traditional notion that Louis Hébert planted grape vines on the slopes above Bear River in the early seventeenth century. He had planned to cultivate some wild grapevines that had been brought to Port Royal, but Marc Lescarbot states in his *Nova Francia* that "by a very dull forgetfulness" this was not done, although the soil appeared suitable. Visitors today, however, will have no doubt that his instincts were correct. The eastern slopes have become a successful grape-growing area. Vines were planted in the late 1990s by the Bear River Winery, and the Annapolis Highland Vineyards opened in 2009. The two vineyards with their wineries overlook the picturesque river valley and welcome visitors.

Just above the town is the L'sitkuk First Nation reserve. A learning centre, health centre, Band Hall, and gas bar, as well as St. Anne's Church, all serve the community. The Mi'kmaq welcome guests to their Heritage and Cultural Centre with its entrance in the shape of a wigwam. The 1.5-kilometre Medicine Trail introduces visitors to the healing plants used in traditional Mi'kmaw medicine, and to other plants of economic value. The L'sitkuk reserve offers us a valuable reminder of its origins and of the many other Indigenous communities that exist today in the traditional territory of Mi'kma'ki.

AFRICAN NOVA SCOTIANS

Nova Scotia's population today includes several Black communities, established by people who were formerly eslaved. The initial wave of Black settlers came to Nova Scotia with the influx of Loyalists who wished to remain under British rule. Among them were hundreds of African Americans who had fought with the British and were rewarded with freedom and promise of land. Some of them were brought to the township of Preston.

Meanwhile, a movement toward the abolition of the slave trade had begun in Britain in the 1780s. In 1786, the British colony of Sierra Leone was created to receive formerly enslaved people who wished to return to Africa. Many of the Black Loyalists seized the opportunity in 1792, and about twelve hundred of them boarded ships in Halifax to take them to their new home.

A second contingent of Black immigrants was the Maroons, who were brought from Jamaica in 1796. They had escaped enslavement and formed independent communities in the Jamaican mountains. When the authorities tried to force their return to the plantations, they fought back in a series of rebellions known as the Maroon Wars, led by Trelawney Town residents, who were the last to hold out. They were eventually captured and punished with exile to Nova Scotia, where they were placed in settlements abandoned by the Black Loyalists. But they had been brought here unwillingly and made no attempt to settle peaceably. In 1800, most of them also left for Sierra Leone.

A third group of African Americans arrived in Nova Scotia after the War of 1812. They were known as the Chesapeake Blacks, because they had arrived on British ships from Chesapeake Bay with the returning British troops.

They had escaped enslavement to join the British side and were seeking a better life in Nova Scotia. They did not necessarily find life easy in Preston and Hammonds Plains where they were given land, but they remained. Many of their descendants still dwell in these communities.

For many years, the poorly equipped schools in Black communities offered minimal education. The Baptist Church became the social heart of each community, providing spiritual and material help to the residents. The history of these settlers is one of tenacity in the struggles against adversity and discrimination, which has resulted in the improvements we see today.

North Preston

North Preston is Canada's largest Black community, and among its oldest. The story of its settlement has several twists and turns. Some Loyalist families brought Black people who were enslaved to them when they came to Nova Scotia in the early 1780s. Black Loyalists—formerly enslaved people who had supported the British in the American Revolution—also came toward the end of the war, between 1782 and 1785. Although some settlers left again as soon as they had the opportunity, others founded Black communities, which survive to this day.

Preston Township was laid out in 1784 by Charles Morris II to provide land for nearly four hundred of these Black Loyalists, or "Free Blacks," as they were known. The township comprised a large area of marginal land in what was at that time a remote location some distance northeast of Dartmouth. It has evolved into a number of discrete settlements, of which North Preston is the most prominent. All Loyalists had been promised land and rations while they established themselves. Most of the white refugees had brought money and goods with them; however, the formerly enslaved Blacks came with very little in the way of material possessions, and many were entirely dependent on government aid once they arrived. Black settlers endured discrimination from the outset. They did not receive the full rations they had been promised. They were forced to work on government projects, for which they were poorly paid. Or they worked as indentured servants, which was little better than what they had escaped.

Although the Black Loyalists had been promised land, the lots they were allocated were smaller than those of their white neighbours. Some received none at all and became tenant farmers in white settlements. And unlike white Loyalists, they were not granted legal title to their land. Instead, they were issued documents known as tickets of location and licences of occupation. This meant they were unable to sell the land, bequeath it to their children, or otherwise dispose of it. Moreover, they could, in theory, be dispossessed of it at any time. Nevertheless, they set about clearing their lots and planting crops. The land they were granted was poor, so it was hard to make a living and feed their families. Winters were harsher than those they were used to, and many became sick. When Black settlers living in Nova Scotia were offered the opportunity to join former slaves in the newly established British colony of Sierra Leone, many of the disillusioned residents of Preston Township chose to escape their miserable conditions and make a new start in Africa.

In 1796, three shiploads of Maroons arrived in Halifax. Faced with the problem of accommodating this new wave of Black immigrants who came with a reputation as troublemakers, Governor John Wentworth hoped that providing them with land would entice them to abandon their rebellious attitude and settle peaceably. He decided to install some of them on the land vacated by those who had left for Sierra Leone, so the population of the community of Preston increased again. The newcomers settled on the farms under similar conditions to those experienced by their predecessors, and they, too, became dissatisfied.

After a while, rebellious factions grew up again, and in addition, the Maroons quarrelled among themselves. A teacher and a chaplain were sent to the community to try to bring about peace, but they had limited success. The Maroons were resistant settlers in Nova Scotia; they had no desire to settle and become self-sufficient here, and they continued to need government assistance to supplement their poor circumstances. They petitioned to leave for Sierra Leone. The authorities eventually decided that the best course of action was to let them go. Almost all the Maroons sailed away from Halifax in August 1800.

The third group of African American settlers in Preston Township was eventually more successful, but their lives were still disproportionately challenging. They were among the formerly enslaved who escaped when fighting occurred around Chesapeake Bay during the War of 1812; they were brought to Nova Scotia as refugees in 1813–14 by the Royal Navy. Between nine hundred and one thousand came to the Preston area, where many of their descendants can be found today. They received land under the same licences of occupation as earlier residents. This arrangement lasted for many generations.

These Black residents of Preston Township were legally free, but they did not enjoy the advantages of white citizens in neighbouring communities. They faced the same discrimination as earlier Black immigrants. As well as problems with land tenure, they had difficulty finding employment and obtaining supplies, among other hardships. They had barely begun to work their farms when "the year with no summer" caused by a volcanic eruption on the other side of the world in 1816 was followed shortly by a plague of mice that destroyed their crops. There was also a threat from forest fires: on June 1, 1918, Lord Dalhousie wrote in his journal that he "went out today to visit the new settlements of the Blacks at Preston, & was glad to find that the fires raging these two days had not done any material damage." But Preston Township, with its poor, rocky soil, was never destined to become a thriving agricultural area. Families struggled to grow sufficient food crops for their own use. Many residents worked at trades within their communities or found employment as labourers or carpenters in Halifax or Dartmouth.

The impediments to obtaining title to their property plagued residents of Black communities from the start, and the situation has persisted for many generations. In 1861, Preston residents still did not have title to the land they were living on, and they petitioned the government to rectify this. Nothing was done, and it would be another century before Premier Robert Stanfield's Land Titles Clarification Act enabled Black individuals to apply for legal title to their property. Only a few families were able to benefit before funding was cut by subsequent governments. Recently, the provincial government's Land Titles Initiative was launched, with the aim of enabling the current residents to finally establish title to their land. In March 2021, appallingly late, a fund was set up to expedite the settlement of claims under this program.

The settlers in Preston brought little with them besides their strong Baptist faith, which helped sustain them through the difficult times they endured and the racism they still encounter. Among the refugees from the War of 1812 was the mother of one of Nova Scotia's most famous preachers, the Reverend Richard Preston. Unlike many of his fellow refugees, young

North Preston's Baptist church can be seen in the background of this old photograph. Now extended, the church remains at the heart of community life.

Richard, a formerly enslaved man of mixed parentage, was literate. He was able to purchase his freedom, and in 1816 he followed his mother to Nova Scotia. Here, the story goes, he found her by chance after knocking on a door in Preston. That door was opened by a woman who turned out to be his mother. He stayed in the community with her until her death and took the name Preston from the community. Richard Preston left to study for ordination as a Baptist minister, and on his return he established the African Chapel in Halifax, later the Cornwallis Street Baptist Church, and recently renamed the New Horizons Baptist Church. He established churches in Black communities across Nova Scotia as he travelled around the province. He founded the African United Baptist Association and campaigned for the abolition of slavery and racism.

The first church in Preston opened in 1842, with Richard Preston as its minister until 1856. At that time, a second church, known as the South Church, was built in what was then known as the New Road Settlement, now North Preston. In 1879, it was replaced with a new building. The present Saint Thomas Baptist Church remains the spiritual heart of the community.

From the late 1880s, the men worked chiefly as labourers. Many women augmented the family income by growing herbs and making baskets and Christmas wreaths, which they sold at the Halifax market. These skills have been passed down through the generations, and are still in use today.

North Preston's first school opened in 1895, with about twenty students from grades primary to eight. It was replaced by a newer school in 1947, which burned down. Nelson Whynder Elementary School, named after a descendant of the Chesapeake refugees, took its place in 1961. These early schools, like many others for Black students, suffered from inadequate provincial support and provided only a limited education. As the population expanded, a second school was built, but Nelson Whynder School was enlarged in 1993 to accommodate all the elementary classes. Older students who attended schools outside the community were often discouraged from pursuing higher education. Fortunately, this is slowly changing, but students from North Preston still frequently encounter discrimination.

The 1970s saw an expansion of community services, including a community centre. A public housing initiative resulted in the construction of new homes. North Preston Medical Day Care Centre opened in 1971, offering medical and daycare programs. A volunteer fire department substation was created in 1976. A new community centre, opened in 2004, provides social and recreational programs, child care, a health and wellness centre, fitness facilities, and a seniors' complex. It also houses an RCMP office. The road out of discrimination is a long one, but in spite of obstacles that persist today, North Preston has forged a strong community spirit.

Upper Hammonds Plains

For many people today, the Hammonds Plains Road is a route rather than a destination. But it was the location of this early road westward from Halifax that determined the growth of the communities of Hammonds Plains and Upper Hammonds Plains. The history of these settlements is also related to Pockwock Lake, a little to the northwest. This was an area frequented for thousands of years by the Mi'kmaq, who fished in its waters, hunted on its shores, and gave the lake its name, said to mean "must stop here" or "can go no further." In summer, they travelled down rivers and lakes to reach their traditional encampment site at the head of St. Margarets Bay, where they spent the summer fishing, gathering molluscs, and trading. There was also an Indigenous land route, a trail that led from Pockwock Lake to the Bedford Basin.

The arrival of settlers altered the traditional way of life for the Indigenous people who lived in the area around Pockwock Lake, including the area that became Upper Hammonds Plains. They lost much of their traditional hunting and fishing grounds to white settlement, logging, and sawmilling, and many of them moved away. Those who remained adopted a more sedentary lifestyle.

In the late 1750s, a road was carved out to link Halifax with the new settlement at Lunenburg. It did not correspond exactly with the present-day Hammond Plains Road, and has been altered over the years, but it followed the same general direction. And as early as 1773, surveyor Elias Wheelock began to mark out a route through the forest from Annapolis Royal toward Halifax. A map made by John Harris in 1784 shows the planned road, ordered by Governor John Parr, which would extend westward from Halifax to Annapolis Royal, passing through Hammonds Plains. It was likely drawn up by sketching a line between the two communities without regard for the intervening terrain, which is rocky and full of lakes and rivers, including Pockwock Lake and the rivers and lakes south of it. The western part of the road from Annapolis was eventually developed as far as New Ross and the road from Chester to Windsor, but the eastern section, intended to join the existing road out of Halifax at Hammonds Plains, was never completed because of the inhospitable terrain. Attempts to revive the project were made from time to time, but without success. A part of it that was constructed beyond Hammonds Plains survives as the Old Annapolis Road hiking trail.

The road from the Bedford Basin to the Head of St. Margarets Bay remained the main route westward from Halifax, and like other early roads, it brought settlers to the area. In 1786, lots were surveyed and laid out by Charles Morris II on land west of the capital. The new community would be known as Hammonds Plains, named after a former lieutenant-governor, Sir Andrew Snape Hamond, and the road running through it became known as the Hammonds Plains Road. But at the end of the century, the "road" itself was still little more than a horse trail and was nowhere near complete.

In 1815, following the War of 1812, some five hundred African American refugees, most of them formerly enslaved, were settled at what became known as Upper Hammonds Plains. They lived along the road now known as Pockwock Road that ran from Hammonds Plains to the foot of Pockwock Lake. The refugees were known as the Chesapeake Blacks, because they had joined the British side on the memorable occasion in 1814 when a contingent of British troops sailed into Chesapeake Bay, marched to Washington, and burned the White House and other public buildings. When they settled in Nova Scotia, the plan to drive the road through to join the existing section from Annapolis Royal was still on the books, and the refugees came to live on what was expected to be part of the main road from the capital to Annapolis Royal.

Like Black settlers in other areas, they did not receive title to their land but were given licences of occupation of ten-acre lots on inferior land that had been abandoned by the white settlers to whom it had originally been granted. They mostly lived in poverty, dependent on government rations and subsidies. As part of the settlement agreement, they were provided with a schoolhouse and a house for the schoolmaster. In the mid-1830s, formal grants were made to thirty residents, affording them title to their property. Others remained unable to sell their land or bequeath it formally to their descendants.

The residents of both Hammonds Plains and Upper Hammonds Plains had remained hopeful that the road to Annapolis would eventually be completed, enabling them to offer services to the passing traffic. Their hopes were dashed in the 1830s, when it became apparent that the impassible terrain would make such a route impracticable, and the plan was finally abandoned. They continued to cut timber, however, and the white community developed a successful lumber industry with mills around Pockwock Lake and other nearby brooks and lakes. Cooperages and woodworking shops in Hammonds Plains produced barrels and boxes, which found a ready market in Halifax. Barrels were in high demand as they were used for local and international shipping of all kinds of goods well into the twentieth century. The population grew considerably during this time. To accommodate the growing community, there were schools and churches, stores, blacksmiths shops, inns, and a Temperance Hall.

The Black residents of Upper Hammonds Plains were not so fortunate. Their land was of poor quality, and life was challenging from the outset. Some of them left for Trinidad in 1821. The remainder made a living as best they

Charlie Symonds of Upper Hammonds Plains, working on a barrel in the 1940s. Barrels were the community's chief product at that time.

could by cutting wood, but poverty was pervasive. They scraped a living from the land, worked for their white neighbours, and caught fish in nearby Pockwock Lake. The more successful among them became coopers.

A Baptist church was established in Upper Hammonds Plains in 1822, and ten years later a second one was opened by the Reverend Richard Preston, the legendary preacher and abolitionist who founded the African United Baptist Association. The two churches combined in 1839 as Emmanuel Baptist Church, and a new building was constructed in 1845. The historic building is still standing, with a major new extension built in 2005, which provides more space for the church's community activities.

A major blow came to Upper Hammonds Plains in 1974, when Pockwock Lake was expropriated, with a derisory sum as compensation, for use as a reservoir to supply water to Halifax and Bedford. A water treatment plant was built on the adjoining land, and water pipes were run through Upper Hammonds Plains. The five hundred or so residents of the community did not benefit from the supply; they still had to draw their water from wells. With the expropriation of the lake, residents also lost their source of fish, their place for swimming, and the spot where their baptisms traditionally took place. But they were resilient; Emmanuel Baptist Church has remained an important spiritual and social centre for the community. The Upper Hammonds Plains Community Centre also provides programs and services for residents, and the community is proud of its all-Black volunteer fire department, the first in Canada.

A notable resident of Upper Hammonds Plains was Madeline Symonds, who in 1828 became the first Black woman to graduate from the Provincial Normal School. She was appointed to teach at the one-room Upper Hammonds Plains School, which accommodated students up to grade nine. As a result of her fundraising efforts, a new school was built in 1945, with more classrooms and new teachers. She became principal. She later returned to the classroom, where she taught grade three. Symonds retired after thirty years of teaching and died in 1996. Her contribution to education in the area is commemorated by the naming of Madeline Symonds Middle School, which serves students from Upper Hammonds Plains and Hammonds Plains.

THE SCOTTISH DIASPORA

Nova Scotia is Latin for New Scotland, the name proposed by Sir William Alexander, Earl of Stirling, when he persuaded King James I to create a new colony in North America. Sir William was a poet and a favoured courtier of King James I of England. He was also enthusiastic about settlement in the New World, and the author of a pamphlet entitled *An Encouragement to Colonies*. In 1621, he persuaded the king to grant him a large area on the Atlantic coast to be known as New Scotland, or Nova Scotia, even though the territory at that time was part of New France and known as Acadie.

In order to settle his proposed colony, Sir William asked the king to create baronetcies for Scots who were expected to finance settlement in this outpost of North America. James I died before this took place, but the project was continued by Charles I. The canny Scots were slow to take up the chance to acquire the title of knight-baronet in return for purchasing land in the new colony, and those who did had trouble finding potential settlers. Even so, a small Scottish garrison on the Annapolis Basin was established by Sir William's son in 1629, while New France was for a short time in British hands. When France regained possession in 1632, the soldiers returned home, and Acadie was left to the French.

Many years later, Sir William's dreams of Scottish settlement here were revived in a way he could not have foreseen. In the late eighteenth century, hundreds of Highland Scots were evicted from their crofts to make way for sheep, in what were known as the Clearances. Many of these Highlanders came to Nova Scotia in search of land where they could make a new start. The eviction of tenant farmers in Scotland continued into the nineteenth century, and more immigrants crossed the Atlantic to join their countrymen. They were not, of course, the only Scots to come here, but within a few years they formed a significant proportion of the population, particularly in Cape Breton.

The Margarees

On Cape Breton's northwest coast, the Margaree River flows into the Gulf of St. Lawrence at Margaree Harbour. It takes its name from the Acadian community established at the estuary of the rivière Ste. Marguerite in the eighteenth century. Many of the communities along the river share the same name, so we find Margaree, where the river narrows, and Margaree Forks where the Northeast and Southwest Margaree Rivers come together. The community of North East Margaree lies on that branch of the river, as do Margaree Centre and Margaree Valley. On the Southwest branch lie Upper Margaree, near the source in Lake Ainslie, and South West Margaree.

For thousands of years, these rivers were a home and highway for the Mi'kmaq, who still have a reserve in the area. The river's rich stock of salmon provided them with a dependable food source and has remained an important part of their culture. As well, there was good hunting in the surrounding forest, where they obtained both food and furs.

With its naturally occurring advantages, the Margaree River became a gateway for European settlers seeking land in the interior of the island. The first of these were Acadians escaping threats of deportation from their homes on the mainland. Some established farms on the lower part of the river. They were followed at the end of the eighteenth century by others, mostly Scots, also in search of land. These pioneers travelled farther up the Margaree, helped by Mi'kmaw guides, to find land they could clear for farming. The Scots came from the Highlands and Islands and would have been happy to see the wooded hills rising above the fertile valleys. Some settled at the place the Mi'kmaq call Wiaqajk, now the community of Margaree, where Indigenous and white inhabitants lived peacefully as neighbours. Another group of settlers continued upriver and turned east at the forks, to a place on the Northeast Margaree that the Mi'kmaq called Mulapukejk, "river gouged out at a spot," where they established themselves. Later, others would follow the Southwest Margaree toward Lake Ainslie.

The scattered settlements along the rivers became home to Scottish families who had left their native land where living was hard in search of places to rebuild their lives. Others had Scottish roots but came to the Margarees by way of Ireland or different parts of Nova Scotia. When they first arrived, these pioneers typically looked for unclaimed land, which they would clear to create farms. They cut down trees to build log cabins for immediate shelter. Planting began with potatoes, which provided some sustenance during their first winter and helped prepare the ground for other crops the following year. Every household kept a few animals. Having claimed and begun to clear their land, they applied for grants to establish title to their property. Surveys were conducted to fix boundaries, and as they received their grants, they settled down to build more permanent homes.

Among the communities established in this way was North East Margaree, which was settled in the late eighteenth century by the four Ross brothers—James, William, Edmund, and David—who were Protestants of Scots-Irish descent. James, the eldest brother, was born in Ireland. He had fought for the British in the American Revolution, was discharged at the war's end, and came from New York to Cape Breton in 1783. In 1787, he applied for a grant of land and initially settled in the Acadian community of Little Bras d'Or, where he met a young widow, Henriette Lejeune. They were married in 1793 and had four children.

Meanwhile, William, the second Ross brother, also born in Ireland, had come to Cape Breton in 1790. He lived first in Washabuck and then Sydney. The two younger brothers, Edmund and David, were both born in Nova Scotia's Hants County, where their parents had settled. They were hoping to join James in Cape Breton, but land at Little Bras d'Or was becoming scarce, so the four brothers decided they would look for good land elsewhere. They stayed for a short time in Little Narrows before continuing their search.

In about 1798, James travelled with Mi'kmaw guides to the valley of the Northeast Margaree. He spent time exploring the area, and here he found a suitable spot for all four brothers to settle. In 1800, he sailed with Henriette and

Clara Dennis visited the Margaree Valley in the late 1920s. Her photograph shows farms along the river and on the hillsides, with the village of Margaree in the distance.

their children from Little Bras d'Or to the Acadian community at Margaree Harbour, and with the help of the Acadians and the Mi'kmaq, set off upriver to their new home. They had brought with them some food supplies, clothing, and domestic necessities, and after a long journey they came to the chosen spot. Here they made a temporary shelter while James cut the trees to build a log cabin. James and Henriette were joined the next year by Edmund Ross and his wife, Nancy, followed by David and William. They obtained adjacent land grants, totalling about 890 hectares.

Many other Irish and Scottish families had also obtained grants in the area in the late eighteenth and early nineteenth centuries. Among them were the Phillips, Cranton, Hart, Ethridge, Ingraham, and Carmichael families. The North East Margaree settlement soon grew into a busy farming community as the population increased. There were abundant trees to be harvested and sawn into lumber in mills on the brooks dropping into the river. There was also excellent salmon fishing in the river.

The salmon fishing began to decline in the later nineteenth century, as sawmills proliferated on the river and its tributaries. Lumbering was an important business, and as the mills flourished the river suffered pollution from mill debris. Fred Veith, an officer appointed to inspect the condition of the Nova Scotia rivers, visited the area in the early 1880s. He noted in his *Report upon the Condition of the Rivers in Nova Scotia*, (1884) that the Marsh Brook, eleven kilometres up the Northeast Margaree, was "much choked with Mill refuse and sawdust." The same was reported of several other brooks feeding the main river, where "sawdust, edgings and slabs, &c., are freely thrown in." Veith concluded, "I am inclined to believe that the cause of salmon not being so plentiful now as in years past in the Margaree and its forks is as much due to the filling up of its tributaries they seek to spawn in with shavings, edgings, slabs, sawdust &c. as it to the poaching with spears and sweep nets at night." Stricter government measures, and the decline of the small sawmills in the twentieth century brought about an improvement to the salmon population. Sport fishing, mandated with catch and release policy, is now an important part of the economy.

The Southwest Margaree River flows out of Lake Ainslie, and the two rivers come together at Margaree Forks. The Southwest River valley was settled by Gaelic-speaking Scottish Catholics. Among the first was Archibald Cameron, who was born on the island of Barra and had fought for the British at Louisbourg. He came to the valley in about 1815. Other early families were the MacDonalds, McLellans, MacDonnells, Gillises, MacFarlanes, and MacDougalls, who obtained grants on the best land they could find. They were joined by settlers from Ireland, who often found that only the less fertile "backlands" were available, and so they had a hard time making a living. As time went on, the distinct communities of Upper Margaree, Gillisdale, South West Margaree, and Margaree Forks developed.

Margaree Forks, home to the Mi'kmaq for thousands of years before settlers arrived, became the site of an Indigenous reserve at the beginning of the nineteenth century. The first European settlers at the Forks were Irish, originating with Myles McDaniel, who came in 1815 and settled just above the reserve. He was joined by others, including three Tompkins brothers—Nicholas, Patrick James, and Michael. The Coady family lived nearby, and descendants of these two families—Fathers Jimmy Tompkins and Moses Coady—are remembered in Nova Scotia for their work as founders of the Antigonish Movement, promoting adult education and organizing of co-operatives as a means of relieving poverty and exploitation.

Like other rural Cape Breton communities, all those on the Margaree were originally based on subsistence farming—a way of life many pioneers had known in their homeland. The new residents supplemented farming by lumbering, and water-powered sawmills were widely established on the region's brooks. The more successful farmers had surplus crops and livestock to sell. Merchants exported the produce and lumber and brought in goods to supply the residents. The abundance of salmon in the rivers attracted well-to-do visitors from other parts of the province and beyond. Fishing lodges were built to accommodate them. These and outfitting provided a boost to the communities' economy.

This way of life continued for much of the first half of the twentieth century. The Second World War and postwar economic development led to young people moving away to make a living in larger industrial or commercial centres. Some left to further their education and never returned. Older people maintained their farms for as long as they could, but the population inevitably decreased.

The tourist industry and the popularity of salmon fishing, particularly in the North East Margaree, continue to contribute to the region's economy. Visitors come from across Canada, the United States, and beyond to enjoy fly-fishing in the river. Descendants of one of the original pioneer families, the Hart family, have done much to promote the sport of salmon fishing. In 2015, the Margaree Salmon Museum at North East Margaree celebrated its fiftieth anniversary. For most of those years, Frances Hart has welcomed visitors, giving them a glimpse of the history of the sport in this community. The hospitality industry has replaced farming as a major source of employment in the area as the Margarees lie on the Cabot Trail, where the spectacular scenery attracts international tourists.

Grand Narrows, Iona, and Little Narrows

The communities of Grand Narrows, Little Narrows, and Iona lie in the middle of the Bras d'Or Lake in Cape Breton, where the Barra Strait connects the northern and southern parts of the lake. Grand Narrows takes its name from its position on the eastern side of the strait, otherwise known simply as the

Narrows. Across the water on the western side of the strait lies Iona, a village on the Washabuck Peninsula. On the far side of this peninsula, the community of Little Narrows overlooks St. Patricks Channel. Grand Narrows is so called because of the width of the strait, as opposed to the far smaller body of water that separates Little Narrows from the mainland.

This was an area well known to the Mi'kmaq, whose name for Grand Narrows was Tewitk, meaning "at the outflow." The Barra Strait served as a passage for their canoes between the north and south sections of the Bras d'Or Lake. Little Narrows was known as Tewitka'jk, "at the small outflow." The Mi'kmaq lived in the area undisturbed by European colonization until the early nineteenth century.

The Scots who settled at what is now the village of Grand Narrows in the early years of the nineteenth century were Roman Catholic Gaelic speakers, who called the place An Caolas Mór. Barra Strait was named by the settlers who came from the island of Barra in the Outer Hebrides, the ancestral home of the McNeils. The first of these settlers was Hector McNeil. He was followed by others from the island, including more McNeils. Like many of their countrymen, they were seeking land and security at a time when farmers in the Highlands and Islands were being displaced to make room for sheep pasture. They cleared land, established farms, cut lumber, and fished in the waters of the Bras d'Or Lake. As the community developed, the residents built a school and installed Archibald McDougall as its teacher. By 1847, a locally operated ferry was running across the strait to Iona. The ferry was later taken over and operated by the Nova Scotia government. In 1851, there was a post office in Grand Narrows, the English name adopted by the community on the eastern shore of the strait. At that time, English was gradually replacing Gaelic as the community's predominant language.

The community's most distinguished son, politician George Henry Murray, was born in 1861 in Grand Narrows, where his parents kept a shop. They left when he was a young child. Murray went on to become a teacher, a lawyer, and eventually the eighth premier of Nova Scotia. He held the latter position from 1896 to 1923, making him the longest-serving head of government in Canadian history.

When the Intercolonial Railway came to Cape Breton in the 1880s, the main line from the Strait of Canso to Sydney ran through the middle of the island. A bridge was built to accommodate the tracks across the Barra Strait from Iona to Grand Narrows, and from there to Sydney. It is the longest railway bridge in Nova Scotia. At Grand Narrows, travellers could transfer between trains and passenger steamers on the Bras d'Or Lake. A large hotel, which is still operating today, was built at Grand Narrows.

The ferry continued to carry road traffic between Grand Narrows and Iona until 1993, when a highway bridge was built across the Barra Strait. Today, there are still McNeils in Grand Narrows, although the population of the community has dwindled. Young people have left to work elsewhere, and some former homes are now only summer residences. The Old Grand Narrows Hotel and the highway bridge to Iona serve the tourist traffic that is now a major contributor to this region's economy. Grand Narrows also has a community-run marina and a café.

The original Gaelic settlers in Iona were also McNeils from Barra. They came in the early 1800s, on the recommendation of Donald "Og" McNeil, who had served with the British army in the mid-eighteenth century and visited Cape Breton. He was impressed by the economic possibilities of this location for farming and fishing. The McNeils were soon joined by other Gaelic families who, like their countrymen across the strait, were Roman Catholics. They named their community Sanndraigh and dedicated their church to Saint Columba. The later name Iona is a reminder of the island of Iona in Scotland's Inner Hebrides, where Saint Columba established a religious community in the sixth century.

The Gaelic language and culture survived in this area of Nova Scotia into the early 1900s, but over the years English became predominant due to its use in schools. As in other rural Cape Breton communities in the twentieth century, farming became less profitable, the traditional way of life paled against outside attractions, and work was hard to find. Iona began to lose its young people, who sought employment elsewhere, but the residents who remained on the island were proud of their Gaelic heritage.

As early as the 1930s, there was talk of creating a replica highland village somewhere in Cape Breton as a way of preserving the Gaelic culture and stimulating the economy, but nothing was done until after the Second World War. In the 1950s, the project was revived, and the people of Iona succeeded in having their area chosen as the site for it. Planning and fundraising followed. Construction started on a small scale in the 1960s, and in the following

The hotel at Grand Narrows, ca. 1891, operated by the McDougalls and the McNeils, welcomed travellers by train and by boat.

decade a master plan was drawn up. More buildings were added to the site in the 1980s and 1990s, and in 2000 Iona's Highland Village became part of the Nova Scotia Museum complex. This resulted in improvements to the genealogy centre that is part of the complex, with expanded interpretative programs and the addition of buildings brought from other sites, including a working carding mill and a church.

Today, the historic village recreates a variety of aspects of the life of early Scottish immigrants. It employs residents of the original community nearby as costumed interpreters to re-enact the daily tasks of these settlers. Women spin, weave, and dye wool, and cook on an open hearth. A blacksmith operates a forge. Men work in the fields. In summer, visitors can enjoy a ceilidh or other cultural events. Visitors may immerse themselves in the Gaelic language and culture of nineteenth-century men and women; Donald McNeil might be surprised to know that the way of life he took for granted is now recreated as part of a museum.

The eastern side of the peninsula, often known as the Iona Peninsula, is separated from the mainland by a smaller body of water, and the community that grew up at the shortest crossing point became known, not surprisingly, as Little Narrows. With a history of Scottish settlement similar to that of its neighbours, the community's later development was influenced by the discovery of large deposits of gypsum nearby in the 1930s. Mining began in 1935, and at its peak, the Canadian Gypsum Company employed as many as 150 people. A conveyor belt carried the gypsum from the quarry to the company's wharf, from which it was exported to the United Sates and other parts of Canada. Business slowed in the early twenty-first century, and workers moved away, although the quarry remained in production with a smaller workforce until the end of 2016. At that time, a drop in demand for gypsum forced the company to wind down operations. It had closed permanently by 2017.

An unexpected find in 2014 carried the history of Little Narrows back to the ice age. Quarry supervisor Lawrence MacNeil found a fossil bone embedded in a newly exposed area. With co-worker Sandy MacLeod and several others, they removed it. The bone was identified as the shinbone of a mastodon that roamed the earth eighty thousand years ago. Remains of these elephant-like creatures are rare in the Maritime provinces.

Little Narrows today is a small, scattered community, accessed from the mainland by a short road branching from the Trans-Canada Highway and leading to the government-operated cable ferry across the strait. From there, travellers can take the scenic Route 223 along the shore to Iona, Grand Narrows, and beyond.

Middle River, Victoria County

Cape Breton's Middle River communities are strung along the scenic Cabot Trail, following the river that runs southward from its headwaters in the Cape Breton Highlands to the outlet on Bras d'Or Lake, west of Baddeck. Middle River flows through the traditional Indigenous territory of Waqmitkuk, which means "clean flowing water." Today, the Wagmatcook Indian Reserve lies at the mouth of the river.

When the first Highland Scots came to the river valley in the early years of the nineteenth century, they were far too busy clearing their land and building their homes to think about a distinctive name for the river. It was simply known by today's prosaic name, which it shares with several others in the province. It is known as Middle River presumably because it bisects this part of northern Cape Breton Island. The settlers established themselves along the valley, forming the long, straggling settlement of Middle River. Groups became centred at spots known as Upper, Middle, and Lower Middle River, further identified as lying east or west of the river. While perhaps lacking imagination, these names at least served as practical guides to their location. The biggest of these communities is Middle River.

Like other Scottish immigrants to Cape Breton, Roderick (Rory) MacDonald and Kenneth MacLeod and their families had left their homeland after the Clearances, when farmers in the Highlands and Islands were dispossessed of their small farms. Unlike their countrymen from Barra, these Gaelic-speaking immigrants from the mainland were staunch Presbyterians. They made their way up the Middle River and began to clear land along its banks, building log cabins and starting a crop of potatoes among the stumps of the trees. They were followed by Peter Campbell and Donald MacRae and their families, who were joined by others until the best land on the river had been taken up. Later arrivals had to make their way into the less productive "backlands" in the surrounding mountains.

Whether they knew it or not, their farms were encroaching on ancestral Mi'kmaw territory where Indigenous people had hunted and fished. Inevitably, tensions arose between the two groups. In 1833, a reserve was designated where Mi'kmaw territorial rights should have been observed, but settlers continued to expand their occupation of the land. In addition to encroaching on Mi'kmaw hunting grounds, the intruders also brought diseases such as tuberculosis and diphtheria to a people who had no immunity to those illnesses. Once a huge reserve comprising 4,500 acres, today's Mi'kmaq community of Wagmatcook has been reduced to just over 700 acres. It was not until the 1980s that a land claim settlement awarded the Wagmatcook band compensation for their loss.

Life was challenging for the Scots who first settled on the river. They had much to learn from the Mi'kmaq about surviving the long winters by hunting and trapping. With only hand tools, they had to clear land, build their homes, and grow food to feed their families. The first crop of potatoes that would form their staple diet helped break up the soil. It was followed by a crop of grain, which was harvested by hand with sickles and threshed with flails until horse-operated threshing mills were introduced. Families kept cows, pigs, sheep, and a few chickens. While the men cut wood and worked in the fields, the women milked the cows, separated the cream, churned the butter, ground the grain with a stone quern, and carded, spun, and wove wool to make clothing, all by hand. Specialized trades developed as blacksmiths and carpenters began to operate. Occasionally, itinerant tailors and shoemakers passed through.

Some activities brought residents together for communal work known as "frolics." The men would assemble for a barn-raising or harvesting; women gathered for quilting and rug-hooking. Both men and women might take part in processing newly woven material by dampening and beating it. This process, known as milling, was accompanied by singing Gaelic milling frolic songs. Some songs brought from Scotland were passed down over the generations. The day's work often ended with an evening of dancing to fiddle music.

All these activities ground to a halt on Sundays, which were strictly observed by the staunch Presbyterians of Middle River, though it would be some time before a permanent resident minister served the community. Visiting clergy came to conduct services and preach from time to time in the 1820s and early 1830s, until finally, in 1834, the Reverend Alexander Farquharson was inducted into the Middle River/Lake Ainslie charge. He came to live in the community of Middle River, where he bought a plot of land and remained for the rest of his life. He was responsible for building the community's first church on his Middle River property.

An event that brought all the Middle River communities together was the annual Communion gathering, held over a period of several days. It began on Thursday with a day of fasting. On Friday, would-be participants were examined by the Elders to determine their belief. Saturday was a day of preparation, particularly for new communicants, all culminating on Sunday, when those deemed sufficiently firm in their faith assembled to receive the bread and wine. On Monday, after a service of thanksgiving, the residents left for their homes. The Communion weekend was an occasion when friends from the scattered villages met and exchanged news.

The Middle River residents suffered setbacks in the 1830s, and again in the 1850s, with the failure of their potato crops. Some of the discouraged settlers opted to join the group of people led by the Reverend Norman McLeod of St. Annes, who migrated to Australia and, eventually, to New Zealand.

As the century progressed, the lives of those who remained were made easier with the setting up of mills on the brooks running into the river. Among the earliest was the sawmill that Donald Nicholson built at West Middle River. More sawmills, a shingle mill, gristmills, and carding mills followed later, enabling residents to replace their log cabins with frame houses, and relieving women of much tedious work. (The carding mill operated by Angus Campbell and Jimmie MacLeod in the 1880s is still functional and has been moved to Iona's Highland Village.) As the population increased, churches, stores, and various services were gradually established in the small communities, and locally funded schools opened.

The area's economy developed with the sale of lumber and farm produce. Village shops supplied many of the families' needs. By the end of the century, the population of the Middle River communities included not only blacksmiths and carpenters but also merchants, tailors, shoemakers, a weaver, stonemasons, and carriage-makers. The early settlers' homes were scattered along the river, and as time went on, they were linked at first by rough trails and later by roads. The main highway on the east side of the river, which has become part of the Cabot Trail, leaves the valley and branches off over Hunters Mountain toward Baddeck. On the west side, a minor road runs through West Middle River toward the Mi'kmaw community of Wagmatcook.

The upper part of the river was caught up in the gold rush that swept Nova Scotia in the 1860s, when it is said that a farmer named Morrison found gold on his property. In 1864, J. G. MacLeod began to work his claim at Gold Brook with several employees. Gold was found along several other streams running into the Middle River, and at the turn of the century an American prospector named Scranton worked with the Great Bras d'Or Gold Mining Company on land that he bought in the area. Scranton later sold his land to the company, which ceased production in 1914 because of labour problems and a dwindling supply of gold.

Over time, many of the farms worked by pioneers and their descendants in the Middle River communities have been abandoned and have reverted to forest, and the population has dwindled as people moved away to seek work in distant places. For many years, each small community on the river had its village school. In 1963, these one-room schools were closed, and children today travel

The Presbyterian and United churches stand side by side in Middle River.

by bus to the Middle River Consolidated School. Village stores have closed, and the remaining residents of the river's communities travel to Baddeck for goods and services.

An old stone house, reminiscent of homes built in the Scottish Highlands, stands on the west side of the river at Upper Middle River. It was built by John MacRae, a member of one of the early pioneer families, in the mid-1880s. It replaced the original log cabin built when the MacRaes first arrived, and remained in the family until 1919. Known today as the MacRae-Bitterman House, it is a registered heritage site. Also in Upper Middle River, on the Cabot Trail, the simple wood-frame MacQuarrie House is another registered heritage building. It was built in 1874 by Donald MacDonald and his son-in-law William MacRae.

Farming and forestry are the central occupations of today's remaining residents, supported by a few small businesses. In the main community of Middle River, two churches stand side by side. One of them is Presbyterian: it was built in 1877 on the site of the original church established by Rev. Farquharson. It is named the Farquharson Memorial Church in his honour. Beside it is the United

Church, a former Methodist building that was brought here from Margaree in 1925 to accommodate the members of the community who favoured church union. The Middle River Consolidated School serves the surrounding area, as does a volunteer fire department. Visitors driving along the Cabot Trail may notice the Scottish family names on side roads that recall the area's Highland heritage.

Earltown

Scots also came to mainland Nova Scotia, beginning with the passengers on the *Hector* who arrived in Pictou in 1773. Some of them ended up in the little village of Earltown, situated on the road running northward from Truro to the Northumberland shore. The area was formerly part of the original Philadelphia Grant that had been awarded in 1765 to a syndicate on condition that it brought in at least a thousand Protestant settlers within ten years to replace the former Acadian residents along the shore. The grant included property on Pictou Harbour, where Scottish settlers took up land along the coast and the river valleys. But much of the interior remained undeveloped. The conditions of the grant were not met, and the unimproved land was escheated and reverted to the Crown.

Governor Wentworth encouraged settlement on the escheated lands, and some of Pictou's Highland Scots encouraged their friends in Scotland to take up the available grants. But these Scots would be latecomers, destined to occupy what were known as the "backlands," with many of the more fertile river valleys already distributed to their countrymen. Among those who responded were Donald MacIntosh and his friend Angus Sutherland. They arrived in Pictou and in 1813 made their way on foot, by way of the West Branch River John, to their new home in what would become the District of Earltown. They constructed a temporary shelter and slept on spruce boughs like the Mi'kmaq hunters, their only neighbours, from whom they were probably able to obtain a supply of meat. They may also have learned from their Indigenous neighbours some of the necessary skills for survival in the forest. MacIntosh and Sutherland set about clearing adjoining patches of land and building log cabins for more permanent homes, to which they would bring wives and children. Only after sawmills were established would they be able to build frame houses. They cut a trail from their cabins to the West Branch to bring in supplies from Pictou.

These pioneers were joined two years later by George and Donald Ross, followed in 1818 by George Matheson. Over the next few years, a surge of immigrant families came from the Scottish county of Sutherland. These included the MacKays, Baillies, Grahams, Murrays, MacDonalds, Munros, among other families. Like the first settlers, they came to Pictou where they stayed with friends while they looked for land to settle in the interior.

By 1836, the area's population had grown to around two hundred people. The early settlers had made their first homes near the West Branch, but as trails, and then roads, extended further, people proceeded to explore the available resources. They quickly spread over quite an extensive area between Nuttby Mountain and West Branch River John. A widely scattered community developed as these Highland Scots found places to make a living from farming and lumbering. The District of Earltown now comprised Earltown Village and West, East, and North Earltown.

The naming of the area presents something of a mystery. It was originally known as New Portugal, because some settlers had fought in the Peninsular War, a conflict over the Iberian Peninsula during the Napoleonic Wars. A survey made by Alexander Miller in 1817 names it Earltown and identifies the satellite villages. The name Earlstown (the early form) is said to have been given to honour the governorship of George Ramsay, 9th Earl of Dalhousie, a fellow Scot, who came to the province in 1817. By 1908, when Deputy Surveyor Gilbert Sutherland made a map of the District of Earltown and part of New Annan, a large number of grants of varying sizes were identified.

From the outset, the economy of the area was based on farming and logging, supported by the establishment of gristmills and sawmills. In 1823, John MacKay established a gristmill on MacKays Mill Brook, around which the village of Earltown grew up. It took thirty-six men to haul two Scottish granite millstones on sleds from the West Branch to the mill. MacKay later added a sawmill and a carding mill. A tannery was operated by Donald MacIntosh's son, John, who may also have run a sawmill. George Henderson and Angus Payne ran blacksmith shops. John MacKay's son Alexander established the Balmoral Grist Mill some kilometres to the north, in 1874. For many years, water-powered sawmills also processed lumber at The Falls, on Waughs River. Farming, however, was challenging in this area, due to shallow soil that was easily depleted. Some of the settlers left in the 1850s and '60s, unable to make a living. Many of those who remained practised trades as well as maintaining their subsistence farms. Some residents were carpenters and builders, and there was at least one shoemaker.

When the roads had improved enough for wheeled vehicles, Alexander Sutherland operated a carriage shop and a carpentry business. Donald Sutherland worked as a carpenter who also ran a farm shop. Robert Baillie practised cabinetmaking and shoe repair. There were other carpenters, as well as blacksmiths and a weaver. Merchants brought in goods and operated stores. Mail for the community was originally brought from Pictou to the home of George Ross, who ran an unofficial post office on a voluntary basis. With improved communications, a regular postal service was established in 1868, and each village in the area had a post office. In those days, a village post office was usually a room in a private home, where people met to chat and exchange news. The first regular postmaster of Earltown was one of the early settlers, William J. MacKay. John MacKay brought the mail from Pictou on horseback.

The first schoolmaster in the area was George Ross, who held classes in his home at North Earltown for ten years from 1827. Earltown Village's first school was a log cabin, replaced in 1830 by another built on land donated by John MacKay. Classes were initially in Gaelic but transitioned to English as communications with the rest of Nova Scotia developed. A new school was built in 1865, after the passing of the Free School Act. It was a standard one-room village school, with one teacher for all grades from primary to eleven.

The early settlers in Earltown had no church. They took their children to Pictou to be baptized or awaited the occasional visit of a travelling minister. They held prayer meetings in their homes until about 1837, when a Presbyterian meeting house was built. Earltown's first minister was the Reverend William Sutherland. During a period when there was a split in the church, two congregations continued to share the building. In the 1860s, they began work on a new building, which opened in 1870. The two groups settled their differences and came together as Knox Presbyterian Church.

By the 1880s, Earltown's population had grown to 350. It was recognized in McAlpine's Directory as a "Post Village." By now, the village served the

Earltown's one-room school, built in 1865, has been repurposed as the village's community centre.

surrounding farming community with two stores, a blacksmith shop, and a gristmill. It was a convenient stopping place at the intersection of the roads that had developed, one to Tatamagouche and the other to River John, and there were two hotels for weary travellers. A rail line brought passengers and goods to the village, and farmers cut wood on their land and hauled it to a railway siding to be transported to purchasers.

The twentieth century marked shifts in the market for lumber as shipbuilding dropped off. In the early 1900s, hardwood from large trees was exported as "ton timber" to English furniture factories. In 1911–1912, John Logan constructed a dam on Earltown Lake where he operated a sawmill, producing hardwood for flooring. After fire destroyed the mill in 1916, Logan and his family left. Logging continued in the area, and portable sawmills were introduced. Even before the railway closed, wood was increasingly transported by truck. From the 1950s, students in grades seven to eleven no longer attended the Earltown School but travelled by school bus to Tatamagouche Rural High School, while the lower grades remained at the village school.

Today, many of the former residents have left, and Earltown is a small rural community of about 250 people. Small as it is, it continues to be the main community of this area of scattered farms. A popular old-time general store, brightly painted and inviting, serves residents and passers-by much as village stores have done for nearly two centuries. Earltown School is still standing, but today all students take the school bus. The building now houses the Earltown Community Centre, home to various activities, including a farmers' market. Earltown Community Church stands at the intersection, with a sign outside inviting passing sinners to repent. The old co-op store is derelict; its site hosts a community bank of mailboxes replacing the former post office. Visitors are attracted to nearby Sugar Moon Farm, where maple syrup is produced and hearty meals are served. There are also hiking and snowshoeing trails at the site. A woodworker in the village produces fine handcrafted furniture, much of which is exported. Earltown today is a community with character.

Caledonia, Queens County

Many visitors to Kejimkujik National Park pass through Caledonia, which lies about halfway along Route 8 linking Annapolis Royal with Liverpool. The centre of the community lies beside Mary Lake, at the intersection with the road to Hibernia. It is the main community in the sparsely populated District of North Queens.

This was Indigenous territory. James F. More, in his *History of Queens County, N.S.*, writes that a man named William Burke was guided by Joseph Gloade, "an extraordinary Indian," on hunting expeditions in this northern district. Returning to Liverpool, Burke recommended the area as suitable for development. In 1798, he led a party of men to blaze a route for the road that was cut through the forest northward from Liverpool and skirted Mary Lake as it continued toward the Old Annapolis Road at Nictaux.

"Caledonia" is taken from the name the Romans gave to Scotland, and reflects the origins of the early residents. In about 1817, eight men came along the road to settle near Mary Lake. Six of them were Scots, with one or perhaps two of them Irish: Alexander Spears, Andrew McLeod, Allen McLean, John Douglas, Richard Telfer, brothers George and David Middlemas, and Edward Hayes. The Scots settled beside Mary Lake at Caledonia and the Irish at Hibernia, the Latin name for Ireland.

Two of the Caledonia settlers were married: George Middlemas brought his wife, Margaret, while Richard Telfer's wife, Mary, is said to have arrived riding on a featherbed on the back of a horse. George and Margaret were the parents of the first child born in the community. The infant was named after his father. Each man chose a drumlin on which to establish a farm. Together they built a log house by the lake, known as the Scotch House, where they all lived while they cleared their land and built their individual homes. As the nineteenth century progressed, other settlers came to the area. One of these pioneers was another Scot, Simon Fraser. He and his wife came from Liverpool in 1830 to Caledonia, where he ran a farm and small business.

Until these settlers arrived, the Mi'kmaq had lived undisturbed on their hunting grounds in this area. They appear to have established friendly relations with the newcomers. In his *History of Queens County, N.S.*, More tells of an early meeting between the settlers and the Mi'kmaq, and also notes the abundance of wildlife that attracted Indigenous hunters to the area: "In 1822, when the first settlers in Caledonia were clearing their land preparatory to farming (on the 10th of March) Joseph Gloade, chief of the Mic-Macs, came to the camp of Patrick Lacey and Thomas Jones, and having got his breakfast returned to the forest. By three o'clock the next day he had killed fifteen moose, though he had at no time wandered more than thirteen miles from the camp." More goes on to describe a powwow that was held at Caledonia in 1836, which "one hundred and thirteen Indians attended. They kept it up the whole week, feasting in plenty." But More observes disapprovingly that by the following Sunday some of them were begging for food.

In 1822, Sir James Kempt, then lieutenant-governor, visited Brookfield and Caledonia, along with the sheriff of the county and other prominent citizens. The party stayed at what More describes as the first public house in the area, run by James Freeman at Brookfield. They had travelled from Liverpool, and Kempt expressed strong disapproval of the road, which the surveyors had blazed in a straight line from hilltop to hilltop. "When the creative hand of the

Supreme Being formed your country," he observes, "he kindly regarded your wants and furnished an admirably level line for a highway through this beautiful and thriving settlement; but you seem to have entirely disregarded a gracious arrangement of Providence which is so palpably indicated." The road was improved over the years, although it was still unpaved in the early twentieth century, when traffic consisted mostly of ox carts and horse-drawn carriages and buggies.

The village of Caledonia grew up around the site of the old Scotch House, but the population did not remain predominantly Scottish, as the original settlers were joined by people from Liverpool and elsewhere. The community grew, and a school, churches, shops, and a bank were established. A Roman Catholic chapel was built in 1836 to serve the Irish at Hibernia. It was later replaced by Saint Jerome's Catholic Church at West Caledonia. Caledonia's Anglican church was constructed in the 1850s. James More records its opening in 1855: "Christ Church, Caledonia, was completed this year (at a cost of £410) and consecrated. The bell was presented by William Sterns, Esq., and a metal communion service by F. W. Collins, Esq. This communion service was burnt in the conflagration at Brookfield, A.D. 1863, (?) [sic] and replaced by a present from the Rev. W. D. Bliss, A.D. 1870. The first service ever held in this church was the burial service over Mr. John Selden, a pious gentleman, at whose instigation the erection of the church was first undertaken." A Baptist church was opened in 1868, and a Methodist church followed at the intersection beside Mary Lake in about 1870. After church union it became what is now the Caledonia United Church.

For many years, farming and lumbering were the main occupations of the residents in and around Caledonia. The community became a major service centre for the District of North Queens. The road passing through it directly from Annapolis Royal—today's Trunk 8—replaced the one through Nictaux as the main route between the Annapolis Valley and Liverpool. The town's services were used not only by the local farming population, but also by travellers, as Caledonia became a stopping place for stagecoaches, with accommodation, meals, stables, and blacksmithing.

The abundant wildlife that had sustained Joseph Gloade and the other Indigenous residents of the area drew sport hunters and anglers and attracted well-to-do vacationers to Caledonia. The Mi'kmaq made a good living by acting as guides for these sportsmen, who stayed at the Alton House, built in 1860. It served as a hotel for many years, and is still standing—one of the last remaining among the fine houses built during this period of prosperity. Another historic home, built by Milton Foster Douglas in 1854, is now a community museum and known as the North Queens Heritage House. Douglas, a successful merchant, operated a lumber mill that was an important part of Caledonia's economy until 1914. Douglas's son, Nelson, inherited the building at the intersection that had housed his father's business headquarters, and operated it as a general store. It remained in the family for many years. In the 1930s, Maurice Scott ran an ice cream parlour and grocery store, as well as a barber shop and a pool hall. The corner store by the lake is still the retail centre of the community.

Toward the end of the nineteenth century, Nova Scotia experienced several gold rushes, as the mineral first discovered at Moose River was found in other parts of the province. In the 1880s, gold mining began in the nearby communities of Whiteburn and Brookfield. Caledonia, midway between the two, became a hub, benefiting from the commercial traffic brought to the area. There was a period of intense activity that lasted into the 1890s; there were stores, hotels, services such as a harness shop, blacksmith shop, a barber shop, and a printing office where a local newspaper, the *Gold Hunter*, was published. Its title reflected the importance of the industry that brought prosperity to the area for some years. Gold mining continued well into the twentieth century but became sporadic. Production slowed, finally coming to a halt as the mineral seams were exhausted.

There was plenty of other commercial activity in the late nineteenth and early twentieth centuries. In the 1890s, Taylor Freeman operated a carpentry business near the corner, producing wheels for carriages and wagons, as well as caskets to supply the undertaker who worked from the same building. Farming, marketing produce, and fruit packing were important facets of the economy. A canning factory processed fruit and vegetables.

In 1904, a railway branch was opened that ran from Bridgewater to Caledonia, replacing the former stagecoach service. By the end of the twentieth century, much of the commercial activity had slowed, businesses closed, and change was afoot. The community is home to a variety of services for the surrounding area, including an elementary school and a rural high school, a post

Alton House, a former hotel in Caledonia, was built in the 1860s and is still standing.

office, a community health centre, a Legion hall, a fire hall, sports facilities, and churches. Travellers will find a visitor information centre and a restaurant. The railway line that once served the community has become part of the recreational Rails to Trails system established on former railbeds. Caledonia has experienced many changes over the past two centuries, but its residents have adapted, continuing to provide services to the population of North Queens and travellers passing through.

View of Prince and Inglis Streets, Truro, Nova Scotia.

3

RIVERS, ROADS, AND RAILWAYS

Three modes of transportation—rivers, roads, and railways—have all contributed to the development of Nova Scotia as we know it today. Rivers served as travel routes for the Mi'kmaq in their birchbark canoes and were also a source of the fish that formed a major part of their diet. The Acadians used tidal rivers to extend their communities inland where they turned the salt marshes along their banks into farmland. For British settlers in the eighteenth and nineteenth centuries, these waterways were exploration routes whereby they penetrated the interior of Nova Scotia in search of farmland. Rivers and brooks were sources of power as well, allowing the establishment of sawmills and gristmills that processed lumber and grain. Water also powered industries such as tanneries and textile mills and provided routes for the export of both manufactured goods and minerals. Inevitably, the province's oldest inland communities depended on rivers for their survival and economic growth.

The earliest roads were rough trails between communities, sometimes based on Mi'kmaw portage routes, and were passable only on foot or on horseback. They were often marked only by blazes on trees, until they had been used long enough to become beaten tracks. They were only gradually made fit for wheeled vehicles. These roads were maintained by statute labour, whereby property owners were required to contribute manpower, along with horses and oxen if they had any, to smooth the surface, fill in holes, remove rocks, and maintain drainage. In the early nineteenth century, stagecoach travel became possible, first on the great roads out of the capital, and later expanding to other routes. Once roads were in place, settlers petitioned for lots along their route where they could start farms and cut lumber. As a region's roads developed, they allowed produce, lumber, and other goods to be sent to market, while merchants used them to bring in supplies to stock their stores. The development of viable roads encouraged the growth of many inland communities.

The coming of railways in the latter half of the nineteenth century gave a boost to the economy of many communities. Goods could now be exported and imported by rail, a faster method than by oxcart or wagon, and train stations became shipping points for farm produce and manufactured items. Freight yards and sidings served local industries, and the railways provided work for local people. The station became the social hub of many a community as farm wagons drew up in the station yard and neighbours exchanged news and gossip as they waited for the train's arrival, bringing mail, freight, and passengers.

Train travel increased mobility throughout the population. While many Nova Scotians had never left the communities founded by their ancestors, it was now much easier than before for people to leave their hometown to seek their fortune elsewhere. The province's population grew more diverse as freedom of movement increased for both native Nova Scotians and new immigrants. Over the years, many Black settlers found employment as porters and waiters on passenger trains.

Now, the railways, too, have had their day, and have been replaced by major highways used by commercial and private vehicles alike. Train lines have been turned into hiking trails. Stations have been demolished or repurposed as museums or restaurants. Nothing stays the same for very long.

ALONG THE RIVERS

Before roads were built, rivers provided access to the interior of Nova Scotia, both for the Mi'kmaq and for Europeans. Fertile land along the river valleys attracted settlers whose initial priority was to be able to feed themselves and their families by subsistence farming. Rivers and the brooks that fed them powered water-driven sawmills that enabled settlers to produce and sell lumber with wood from the surrounding forest. The rivers continued to provide transportation for many years, even after roads were established, as they were a means of exporting heavy materials like coal and lumber as well as providing travelling routes that were often preferable to rough land passages. Although rivers were valuable for development, they also posed obstacles to travel as inland settlements took hold. Initially, fords and ferries served to link opposite sides. Bridges eventually replaced them, and communities grew up where roads converged at these sites.

Settlers toiled to clear land to build a home and establish crops. Trees had to be felled with axes and saws, and ground prepared with hoes. Once a suitable place was found, often along a river, they could apply to the provincial authorities for a formal grant. At first, some food supplies had to be brought in. Fish from the river and game from the forest supplemented their diet, but eventually subsistence farms grew up that made the settlers self-sufficient. When British settlers came to a valley and began to clear land for farming, they encroached more and more on the ancestral Indigenous hunting grounds, frequently causing acrimony among people who had previously welcomed and assisted newcomers.

Waterfalls and rapids in the rivers and brooks provided power to operate sawmills, which enabled frame houses to replace the original log cabins, and formed the basis of a lumber industry that sustained the economy of many riverside communities. The rivers themselves provided transport routes to get logs to the mills and finished lumber to the coast for use in shipbuilding or for export. Communities developed as people came together to build schools, churches, stores, and other services, and often to develop other natural resources in the area.

The Musquodoboit Valley

"Musquodoboit"—a name that visitors to the province have difficulty pronouncing—is the anglicized version of the Mi'kmaq name Muskoodeboogwek. Its meaning is uncertain. I have come across three completely different translations, but all refer to the river of the same name that served as a highway for the Mi'kmaq, and along whose banks they made camp.

The Musquodoboit River flows from northeast to southwest along a valley between Glenmore Mountain to the north and lower hills to the south, running parallel to the coastline, before turning sharply southward to the sea. Small communities are found along the valley; three of them take their names from the river: Upper, Centre, and Middle Musquodoboit. The little town at the mouth of the river, predictably known as Musquodoboit Harbour, is beyond the scope of this book.

According to the Acadian census of 1707, "Mouscouadabouet" had a Mi'kmaw population of 161. These figures were presumably based on the number of people who lived and hunted in the forest along the river valley. They probably traded with Acadians, who did not seem to venture beyond the harbour.

In 1784, seven men with their families came to the upper reaches of the Musquodoboit River as they were making their way from Truro toward St. Marys River, where they had intended to settle. Instead, they liked what they saw at their stopping place and decided to stay. Their names were James, John, and Samuel Fisher, John Holman, Robert Geddes, Stutely Horton, and Thomas Reynolds. They cleared land and established farms at what became Upper Musquodoboit. The area was originally known as the Fisher Grant. It consisted of over 5,300 acres. These pioneers were tough. Before a local gristmill was built, Stutely Horton is said to have carried a bag of wheat probably weighing about twenty-seven kilograms from Upper Musquodoboit to Truro to be ground.

The settlers were joined in 1785 by George Farnell, who had fought in the American Revolution. He married John and Elizabeth Fisher's daughter, Margaret. Ten years later, James Dean and his family arrived from Britain. In 1819, as lieutenant-governor, Lord Dalhousie recorded his visit to "the furthest settlement in Musquodoboit" where he met "a little old man by the name of Deans [sic], [who] had been a gardener in his early days. He is very happy in a nice farm where he raises hops in great perfection & proves that they might be cultivated to any extent in Nova Scotia." Lord Dalhousie did not record what was done with the hops, but no doubt Dean and his friends enjoyed their beer.

The nineteenth century saw new arrivals. A second group of settlers came to Upper Musquodoboit from Truro in 1825, carrying grain, seed potatoes, and other supplies more than fifty kilometres through the forest over rough trails. One early grantee, William Annand, was a Halifax merchant who acquired land at Upper Musquodoboit. Annand was elected to the provincial assembly for the Reform Party in 1836, following the leadership of Joseph Howe in the Reform movement. Howe spent two years with Annand in Upper Musquodoboit, where it is said that he was a popular figure. In 1843, Annand left politics, bought the *Novascotian* from Howe, and became a publisher. He left his land to his two sons, William and James, who ran a cattle farm and built a fine house there.

As the community expanded over the years, churches, schools, and stores were established. In 1915, a railway line reached Upper Musquodoboit, and the first train arrived early the following year, allowing for timely export of the farm produce. For many years, logging has contributed to the economy, but the lumber industry introduced problems as well as benefits. In early years, the settlers along the valley were able to enjoy fish from the river. As time went on, a dam constructed for a sawmill near the mouth of the river impeded the upstream passage of fish. A long-time resident told fisheries inspector Fred Veith in 1881 that "immense quantities of salmon, shad, sea trout and gaspereaux" had once made their way up the river, but since the construction of the dam, there were very few fish to be found. It is not known what impact Veith's report had on the sawmill operation. In the twentieth century, pulpwood became an important product, and today, a pellet mill is operated by Great Northern Timber at Upper Musquodoboit.

Two other communities in the Musquodoboit Valley take their names from the river: somewhat confusingly they are called Middle and Centre Musquodoboit. Middle Musquodoboit was earlier known as Middle Settlement, then Laytonville. In the 1800s, Centre Musquodoboit was called Deacontown. In the early 1780s, William Guild came from Scotland to Nova Scotia, and became the first white settler in what is now Middle Musquodoboit, a place that the Mi'kmaq called Natkamkik, "the river extends up hill." From that time on, the Indigenous inhabitants would increasingly find their territory taken over by settlers. Guild cleared land and built a log cabin, where he was joined the following year by his wife, Jessie, their three sons and two daughters. He was among the pioneers in the valley who received grants in 1787. As soon as he could, he replaced the log cabin with a frame house. Around 1800,

The centennial of the Presbyterian church was celebrated at Dr. Harrison's home in Middle Musquodoboit in 1915.

he drowned in the river. His son William built a new home, moving the old house further back and using it to store wood. He worked as a farmer, as did his brothers James and Matthew.

Among other early settlers was John Layton, who was born in Falmouth in 1777. He arrived as a young man in about 1801 with his new wife, Catherine. He was the son of a blacksmith, and he practised the same trade. He and his wife had twelve children, one of whom died in infancy. Not all of them remained in the community, which took the family name for a while, but their fourth son, Francis, followed the family pattern and worked there as a blacksmith. William, the sixth son, operated a store. We know that at least two of their daughters remained in Middle Musquodoboit. Mary was married to John Bates, a farmer, and Letitia's husband, William Harrison, was a physician.

Dr. Harrison, who emigrated from England in 1830, not only cared for his neighbours but also attended Mi'kmaw patients, for which he was paid by the government on a fee-for-service basis. He built a fine house in Middle Musquodoboit. John Layton gave the land on which the Presbyterian church—the first in the community—was opened in 1815. It celebrated its centenary with a gathering at Dr. Harrison's residence.

The population of Middle Musquodoboit increased in the nineteenth century as more settlers arrived. The first school was established in 1817. According to the 1838 census, there were 871 people living there at that time. Most of them were farmers, but there were also blacksmiths, carpenters, millers, a shoemaker, a parson, and a number of schoolmasters. Colonel Henry Arthur Gladwin, JP, who lived on La Prairie Farm, was identified in the census as "Justice, Farmer." He was born in India, educated at Eton and Cambridge, had served in the British Army in India, and came to Canada as military aide to Sir John Sherbrooke. He bought La Prairie Farm, where he lived with his wife and a large household. He seems to have led the life of a country squire. Holy Trinity Anglican Church was built in 1830 on a portion of his land. He was laid to rest in 1881 in the family plot in the church cemetery, at the age of ninety.

Middle Musquodoboit was a busy place in the nineteenth century: initially, stagecoaches stopped there to deliver mail, passengers, and freight; there were several hotels, a post office, and banks. In 1916, when the railway was opened, a train station replaced the former stagecoach stop. The line remained in service until the early 1960s. Although by the early twenty-first century the population had declined to 669, Middle Musquodoboit remains at the heart of an agricultural community. It is the home of the annual Halifax County Exhibition, and its hospital and rural high school serve the entire valley.

Midway between Upper and Middle Musquodoboit is Centre Musquodoboit, which was part of a large grant given to John, Matthew, and Robert Archibald from Truro. Some members of the Archibald family established a small community. "Little Will" Archibald operated a tannery and harness shop. After the tannery closed, the harness shop was operated by P. G. Archibald, who later converted it to a store. A school named for the Archibalds was opened in about 1869. When the railway came to the valley, it brought goods for P. G.'s store to what was known as Archibald's siding. The railway provided a means for local farmers to export their produce and served the local lumber industry generated by sawmills operating in the area. A fire in 1918 was a serious blow to the community.

Today, Centre Musquodoboit is a dot on the map in a forestry and farming area that you might drive through unaware of its existence. The fertile land that attracted the early settlers to the Musquodoboit Valley still supports agriculture. The small family farms that pioneers once worked by hand have given way to larger, mechanized operations. and lumbering is still carried on.

The Stewiacke Valley

In the fall of 1880, residents of the Stewiacke Valley were preparing to celebrate the one hundredth anniversary of settlement on the Stewiacke River. A commemorative booklet entitled *Celebration of the 100th Anniversary of the Settlement of Stewiacke! Held on October 6th, 1880* was published afterwards. It describes the proceedings that were centred on the Upper Stewiacke Presbyterian church, its grounds, and an adjacent field. Guest speakers were invited, the church was decorated, an arch was built over the entrance to the field, where tables were set out for a thousand or more participants, and the women of the communities were busy preparing food. The Truro brass band was engaged, and a large choir was formed. But October 6 turned out to be what was described as "the most stormy and disagreeable day of the season." Outdoor ceremonies, according to the commemorative booklet, were out of the question.

Despite the weather, the event was well attended: "From 8 o'clock till 12 one continuous procession of carriages from all directions poured into the village, until by one o'clock, over 2,000 people were on the grounds." The ceremonies took place in the church, which normally could seat a little over 1,000 people, and on that day over 1,500 squeezed in. Attendees offered prayers, sang hymns, and listened to addresses given by church and civic dignitaries. In the interval between speeches, neighbouring families opened their homes where the ladies who had prepared tea served as many people as possible indoors before the proceedings continued. The speeches presented a vivid picture of pioneer life in the Stewiacke Valley. One speaker predicted that "the echo of [the voices of the participants] will roll along, through the succeeding years, and re-echo at Stewiacke's next Centennial."

The history of the Stewiacke Valley goes back for many more than one hundred years. The Mi'kmaq knew the Stewiacke River as Sesiktewiaq, which has been interpreted in several ways, perhaps meaning "winding river." Flowing into the Shubenacadie River, it was a travel route giving access to both the Bay of Fundy and the Atlantic Ocean. When British settlers came to the area, the Mi'kmaq lived alongside them and continued to fish in the river and hunt in the forest.

The site of Lower Stewiacke, now simply Stewiacke, was first populated sometime in the early 1700s, when fourteen Acadians reclaimed marshland for farming at the confluence of the Stewiacke and Shubenacadie Rivers, forming the community of Ville Pierre Hébert in Matthieu Martin's seigneurie of Cobequid. Martin died without heirs in about 1724, and his extensive grant east of the Shubenacadie passed to the British Crown in 1732. The Acadians remained on their farms for a while. A map by Captain Lewis made in the early 1750s shows the Village Hébert, but relations with the British had deteriorated, and by the time of the deportation they had already left for Île St-Jean, now Prince Edward Island.

During the French and Indian War (1754–1763), plans were made to build a fort on the former Acadian land as a defence against the Mi'kmaq. Fort Ellis was completed in October 1761, but by that time Peace and Friendship Treaties were already signed, and the fort was redundant. It was never garrisoned and was completely abandoned in 1767. British settlers eventually took over the flat farmland around Fort Ellis. There were no tumbling brooks suitable for operating a water mill, so in 1834 George Burgess received a grant to build a windmill to process the local farmers' grain. Much of the farm work was still done by hand, but when a farm property at Fort Ellis went up for sale in 1841, the equipment included a horse-operated threshing machine.

The introduction of steam mills in the latter part of the nineteenth century provided a more dependable source of power. In 1890, Alfred Dickie and Avard Black established a lumber mill in Stewiacke, using a horse-drawn pole railway to transport logs to the mill. By the early twentieth century, the Dickie Company of Stewiacke was among the leading lumber companies in the province, with mills in several other locations.

Stewiacke's main residential area grew up on the south side of the Stewiacke River. Its original Baptist church was founded in 1832. The present building dates from 1924. Holy Trinity Anglican Church was built in 1909, but since the parish combined with that of Shubenacadie, the historic building has been repurposed as an Airbnb. Today, the town is the valley's largest community, with its town hall, legion hall, and a variety of businesses serving the surrounding area. Its Mastodon Ridge Park commemorates the discovery of mastodon bones at a nearby gypsum mine.

Settlement along the valley began in 1780, when New Englander William Kennedy came from Truro, cleared land, and established a farm at Middle Stewiacke. Kennedy was joined by Samuel Teas, David Fisher, Simeon Whidden, and others. Over the next few years, more settlers received grants. The Stewiacke Valley was traditional Mi'kmaw territory, and an interesting petition from William McCurdy in 1785 requested a grant of land on the Stewiacke River "next to Paul the Indian," confirming the continued presence of the Mi'kmaq as neighbours.

Soon after they arrived, the settlers began to explore farther upriver, where they came upon an area that appeared particularly fertile and well-suited for farming. When this news reached Truro, John Harris and fifty other potential settlers applied for and received a grant in 1783 at what would become Upper Stewiacke. Not all the recipients took up their land, but in the fall of that year, Matthew Johnson came from Truro and built a home for himself and his wife, Ruth. At first, they were the only white settlers, but they had no fear of their Indigenous neighbours. Records show that the newcomers and the Mi'kmaq of the Stewiacke Valley lived peacefully side by side. One of the speakers at the Centenary, quoted in *Celebration of the 100th Anniversary of the Settlement of Stewiacke! Held on October 6th, 1880*, observed that the Mi'kmaq were "of a peaceable and friendly disposition...to those whom they considered as intruders on their soil."

The Johnsons were joined the following year by William Fulton, Samuel Fisher, Charles Cox, Thomas Crocker, and Samuel Taylor. Within two years, John Archibald, Samuel Creelman, and Richard Upham had also arrived. This was the beginning of what would become the leading community on the upper river.

By 1817, Lord Dalhousie observed in his journal that there were "thriving new settlements" on the "Souiac" river, but the lives of the early settlers had not been easy. Although sawmills allowed the construction of frame houses, well into the nineteenth century most of the homes in the valley were still built of logs that had been cut by the earliest settlers. The land was fertile and their farms productive, but before roads were built, farmers had difficulty getting their produce to market. It had to be taken down the Stewiacke River by boat, then either down the Shubenacadie to Truro or upriver and through Grand Lake to Fletchers Lake. From there, the bags of produce were taken along a trail to Halifax, slung on the backs of horses. Supplies from the capital were carried back in the same way along the same circuitous routes. Once a road was built in the early 1800s, this last leg of the journey was completed by wagon.

In early days, the nearest gristmill was in Truro. Wheat was sent there by boat or canoe for grinding, and flour was brought back the same way, or it was carried on a man's back through the woods. The story was told of a man who carried a bushel bag of flour on his back from the gristmill at Truro and was so exhausted by the time he reached the river that he sat down to rest before crossing, fell asleep, and awoke only after sunrise the following morning. Life became easier after William Putnam built the community's first gristmill. Farmers still had to carry grain and flour on their backs to and from Putnam's mill, but at least it was a much shorter distance.

The Stewiacke Valley settlers were staunch Presbyterians, but for some years the communities had no resident clergy. Occasionally—sometimes at intervals of years—visiting Presbyterian ministers from Truro, Londonderry, or Pictou conducted services in private homes. A small log church was built in Upper Stewiacke in 1793. A frame building later replaced it. The Reverend James Munroe, the first minister appointed to the area, served both Upper and Middle Stewiacke, as well as Onslow and Musquodoboit. The first resident minister, the Reverend Hugh Graham, was appointed in 1800. He lived in Upper Stewiacke and served both Stewiacke communities. A meeting house was built in Middle Stewiacke around 1812, but it burned shortly after completion. Its replacement served until 1847, when in turn it was replaced by a larger building. That same year, Middle Stewiacke welcomed its own minister. By 1880, there was also a Baptist congregation at Upper Stewiacke.

The nineteenth century was a period of development. By 1814, there were sixty-four families living in Upper Stewiacke, which grew faster than Middle Stewiacke where there were only twenty-two families. From those early days, Upper Stewiacke has remained the social and commercial centre of the

The former Upper Stewiacke Community Hall, built in 1886, now serves as the Stewiacke Valley Museum, with a fine collection of items from the area.

Stewiacke Valley. Initially the farmers grew potatoes and wheat and raised pigs, but by the 1820s the once-rich soil of the valley farms was being depleted from constant cultivation. Yields of wheat and potatoes declined, and oats replaced them as the chief crop. In 1822, John Gourley built an oat mill. Logically, oatmeal became a standard part of the residents' diet. The roads were improving, so wagons and buggies gradually came into use. A weekly mail service was introduced in about 1823. When Joseph Howe visited in 1829, he observed in the posthumously collected sketches titled *Western and Eastern Rambles* that the valley was "in many places highly cultivated and extremely productive… sending forth to the capital fine quarters of beef, very superior mutton, and lots of pigs and poultry." By the time of the centenary, the farms were prospering, and sawmills, gristmills, shingle mills, a dyeing works, a woollen factory, and a quartz crusher were operating on the brooks in the area and on the South Branch of the river.

During the twentieth century, local industries closed, diversified, or gave way to operations in larger centres. As roads improved, farm produce was carried away and goods were brought in by truck. Residents exchanged their buggies for cars in which they drove down the river to Stewiacke and beyond. The Presbyterian churches in both communities joined the United Church of Canada. This was still farming country with agriculture at the heart of the economy. In 1983, the speaker's prophecy of 1880 was fulfilled when another celebration was held to commemorate the 200th anniversary of Matthew Johnson's arrival in Upper Stewiacke; a re-enactment took place, and a monument was unveiled. Today, both Upper and Middle Stewiacke are comfortable farming communities. The fine little Stewiacke Valley Museum in Upper Stewiacke's Community Hall is operated by the local historical society, which strives to preserve and present the history of the valley.

The Grand Lake Communities: Wellington and Oakfield

Shubenacadie Grand Lake, often known simply as Grand Lake, is at the head of the Shubenacadie River. On the eastern shore of the lake is a large rock that held great significance to the Mi'kmaq, who for thousands of years lived and travelled on the lake they called Kji-qospem. The rock is identified on modern maps as Indian Point, a rocky headland jutting into the lake in Oakfield Provincial Park. The Mi'kmaq of the Sipekne'katik First Nation honoured it as Grandmother Rock, a traditional stopping place on the water route from Kespukwitk (Chebucto, now Halifax Harbour) to their community at Sipekne'katik (Shubenacadie), where they could pull up their canoes and pause for rest and shelter. Grandmothers are honoured in Indigenous tradition as guides and protectors.

After many years of sporadic outbreaks of hostilities between the Mi'kmaq and British settlers, Peace and Friendship Treaties were signed in 1760 and '61. The Mi'kmaq continued to exercise their rights to hunt and fish around the lake, but as time went on, settlements began to encroach on their hunting grounds. In 1779, a reserve was created by the colonizers on the western side of the lake, but it represented only a small portion of the former Mi'kmaw territory.

British settlement began on the east side of Grand Lake, where William Shaw received a grant of two thousand acres in 1784 around what is now Wellington. He was joined by other grantees James Oram, John Lees, and John Gay. William Fletcher bought land at the northern end of what became known as Fletchers Lake from Halifax merchant Peter McNab. Fletcher in turn sold some of this land to his son, Robert, who made his home there in 1795.

In the late eighteenth century, a trail ran from the head of the Bedford Basin on the western side of the lakes to the southern end of Grand Lake, where it crossed Fletchers Bridge. This was a transshipment point: boats brought produce from farms along the Shubenacadie and Stewiacke Rivers to be taken through the lake and overland to Halifax along a rough trail to the head of the Bedford Basin. The trail was improved in the early nineteenth century to become Cobequid Road, usable by wheeled vehicles. This was the second of Nova Scotia's great roads, and the precursor of Trunk 2. In about 1815, Robert Fletcher opened an inn beside the bridge, which for many years was a welcome stopping place for travellers. When a stagecoach route was established along the Cobequid Road in 1816, coaches stopped at Fletcher's Inn to discharge and take on passengers, mail, and packages.

As early as 1797, the assembly had approved the first survey for a canal that would link Halifax Harbour with the Shubenacadie River; however, the project would take many years to come to fruition. The survey identified places where water levels dropped between the lakes along the route, creating descents that would impede navigation. The Mi'kmaq had established portages around such obstacles, but these were not practicable for larger vessels. Locks would have to be built. Further surveys caused delays and work did not begin on the Shubenacadie Canal until 1826.

There would be locks at both ends of Fletchers Lake: Lock 4, known as Fletchers Lock, at the south end, and Lock 5 at the entrance to Grand Lake. Granite from the quarry on the west side was used to build the walls of the two locks. Lock 5 was 43 metres long, 5 metres wide, and almost 7 metres deep. During its construction, which began in 1828, as many as thirty labourers and masons lived at the site. On the east side was a shipyard where steamers and barges were built for use on the canal, and there was also a mill. When Joseph Howe's stagecoach stopped at Fletcher's Inn as he journeyed to Truro in 1829, he noted, in the collection *Western and Eastern Rambles*, the construction site as "the ground intended for one of the locks of the Shubenacadie Canal."

The building of the canal was fraught with labour and engineering problems, and there were many more delays, but in 1856 the locks on Fletchers Lake were finally operational. By 1858, a few vessels, including a steamer service, began to pass through them into Grand Lake. The first steam vessel was a sidewheeler, followed by two sternwheelers, and a barge that could be towed but also had sails that allowed it to travel under its own power. Cargoes included heavy materials such as lumber, bricks, and granite. The operation of the locks was overseen by a lock-keeper, William King, who lived at Lock 5. For a time, the area around his home was known as Lockport, but Fletchers Bridge was a well-known landmark and the name persisted. In 1861, the final stage of the canal, the inclined plane at the Dartmouth end, was completed and the first traffic between Halifax and the Minas Basin, including steamships, freight scows, a barge, rafts, and Mi'kmaw canoes, passed through the locks. Meanwhile, a community was developing beside Fletchers Bridge, which would later be known as Wellington.

The idea of a canal was a good one in its day, but by the time it was finished changes to infrastructure had already taken place that would make it redundant. The Nova Scotia Railway had begun to operate in 1858, providing a faster and more efficient mode of transportation, and the rail bridges that crossed the canal were too low for a steamer to pass underneath. Use of the canal dropped off quickly, and it soon fell into disrepair. The locks deteriorated until Mi'kmaq canoes were the only craft that passed under the bridges. Today, some restoration has taken place along the canal, and modern-day canoeists enjoy paddling the former Mi'kmaw travel route.

The community of Oakfield came into being in 1865, when Major John Wimburn Laurie came to Nova Scotia after serving in the Crimean War. He purchased a large tract of forested land on the eastern shore of Grand Lake, including the headland known as Indian Point where the Grandmother Rock was located. He built a house on the estate, which he named Oakfield, where with his wife, Frances, he raised a family. While pursuing his military career, he brought in tenants from England to clear and farm the property and established a sawmill and a tannery. The Oakfield model farm was noted for its Guernsey cattle.

Laurie built cottages and a church for his employees, and a school for their children, forming the basis for the present community of Oakfield. He seems to have been a benevolent employer: when farm workers retired, they were given ownership of their houses. Laurie became warden of Halifax County in 1880, and it was he who gave the name Wellington to the community at Fletchers Bridge, in honour of the hero of the Napoleonic wars.

The Intercolonial Railway line ran along the east side of Grand Lake, and stations were built for its communities: Wellington Station was at the southern end of the lake, and Grand Lake Station served the Oakfield estate. The stations have long gone, but both names have survived as locations along Trunk 2.

When John Wimburn Laurie left the army with the rank of lieutenant-general, he continued to operate the farm. He held several public offices, and entered politics, representing Shelburne in the House of Commons from 1887 to 1891. In 1889, he returned to England, where he died in 1912. His wife returned to Oakfield, where she spent the rest of her life.

One of the Lauries' sons was killed in the Boer War and another in the First World War. The property at Oakfield was inherited by their only surviving son, Kendrick Cartaret Laurie, who lived there and continued to maintain it like a benevolent feudal lord of the manor. He was frequently absent on military duties, serving in the Boer War and in the First World War. On retiring in 1922, he returned to Oakfield with his wife, Violet Boardman, to supervise the farm and the affairs of the community until his death in 1967. Mrs. Laurie continued to live in their house, and to maintain the tradition of giving their houses to retired employees. She entertained members of the community. C. Morrison remarks in personal communication, "We were given a wonderful roast lamb meal—Mrs. Laurie said it was one of their last ones. She did not give us a tour of the property but did give us a tour of the house. She was proud of a dumb waiter her husband had installed."

After Mrs. Laurie died in 1984, leaving no children, changes crept in to Oakfield. The same community member recalls that a relative, Michael Laurie, took over the property. His wife ran the old cattle barns as a horse barn. There were remains of a metal system for transporting milk, as the farm had been

Lock 5 at Wellington, between Fletchers Lake and Grand Lake, photographed by Clara Dennis in the 1930s. Note the drop in the water. Today, the lock has been restored.

highly mechanized for its time. When it ceased to operate, the former workers either retired or began to work in the city. The church dedicated to St. Margaret of Scotland, once privately owned by the Lauries, became part of the Diocese of Nova Scotia. Members of the Laurie family and other early residents of Oakfield are buried in its graveyard.

The Oakfield estate passed to the Province of Nova Scotia and the former farmland and surrounding woods became two provincial parks, Laurie Park and Oakfield Park. They are now popular recreation areas with opportunities for swimming and boating on Grand Lake. Laurie Park provides camping facilities, while Oakfield Park is an accessible picnic park which also features a multi-use trail that winds around Indian Point, bringing its users to the spot where once the Mi'kmaq beached their canoes under the protection of the Grandmother Rock.

The Shubenacadie Canal and locks lay derelict for many years, but in the 1980s, their restoration began. Lock 5 was the only one to be fully restored, using the original stones, and it is now a Provincial Historic Site. Visitors to Lock 5 Park can see the lock itself, and the foundation of lock-keeper William King's house. An interesting period of Nova Scotia's history is recreated here.

ALONG THE ROADS

While some of the earliest inland communities had grown up along rivers, the establishment of roads opened many more areas for development. The first roads that were cut into the interior also brought settlers, who in their turn cleared land for farms. Settlers often gathered near brooks that were a source of both fresh water and power for saw- and gristmills. The early roads were often primitive trails, but they allowed would-be settlers to make their way on foot, or if they were fortunate, on horseback, to find land in the interior of the province where they could make a living. When roads became passable for wheeled vehicles, communities along their routes offered travellers lodging, refreshment, a change of horses, and blacksmith's services.

The two great roads linking Halifax to Windsor and Truro were the first where, from the early nineteenth century, wheeled vehicles could travel in summer and be replaced in winter by horse-drawn sleighs. Like the settlers along the rivers, people were looking for land where they could make a living with subsistence farming and perhaps grow a crop to send along the road to market. Some entrepreneurs acquired large grants that they subdivided and sold or rented out to tenants. Communities grew up where neighbours came together to build barns, schools, and churches, and merchants set up shop and brought in supplies. As more roads were built in the nineteenth century, the population of inland Nova Scotia slowly increased.

The Sackvilles

The sprawling communities of Upper, Middle, and Lower Sackville can trace their origins to a time shortly after the foundation of Halifax in 1749, when a fort was built at the mouth of the Sackville River, situated at the head of the Bedford Basin, to defend the new settlement against attack by the French and their Mi'kmaw allies. It is said that the fort also served to intercept potential deserters from the Halifax garrison. The river and fort were named after British politician George Germain, 1st Viscount Sackville. The name became attached to the first community that grew up beside the river. In early days, this included the area around the fort and extended for some distance along the road now known as the Old Sackville Road.

The area at the head of the Bedford Basin had been home to the Mi'kmaq for thousands of years. Petroglyphs carved in the rock at their traditional gathering place near the mouth of the Sackville River, now known as the Bedford Barrens, are testament to their presence in what continues to be for them a spiritually significant site. The British construction of Fort Sackville on their territory was naturally a cause for resentment. Armed confrontations took place, with casualties on both sides. Fort Sackville was manned by a New Englander, John Gorham, and his Rangers who were mostly Indigenous fighters from Gorham's home in Cape Cod, and who were merciless in their pursuit of the Mi'kmaq.

Fort Edward was established in Windsor. Communication between the two forts was by way of what was known as the Pisiquid Trail, which ran alongside the Sackville River. Originally established by the Mi'kmaq, the trail had been used by the Acadians to drive cattle to Chebucto (Chebouctou, as the French knew it then) for export to Louisbourg. The trail was improved in the early 1750s, largely by Acadian labour, to create a military road between Halifax and Windsor. The road was the scene of another cattle drive after the Expulsion, when the Acadians' livestock was dispersed to farms around Lunenburg. By the early nineteenth century, the former trail had become Nova Scotia's first "great road."

Near Fort Sackville was the estate of Joseph Scott. This entrepreneur acquired extensive lands at the head of Bedford Basin, where he built saw- and gristmills on the river and established a profitable lumber business. The home that he built in the 1770s, Scott Manor House, was the first in the area and it still stands. He built an inn on the road, Ten Mile House, which is also extant though it was moved back from its original location when the road was widened. Scott fell on hard times, and his last few years were a struggle for survival. He died in 1800, and his home became the residence of William Sabatier, a Halifax merchant. Sabatier left for England in 1819, and the house changed hands several times until the late twentieth century, when it became a community museum known as Scott Manor House.

The opening of the great road to Windsor was followed by a second one that branched off toward Cobequid (now Truro) a few kilometres beyond Fort Sackville. Today, they are known respectively as the Old Sackville Road and the Old Cobequid Road—the forerunners of Trunks 1 and 2. The Old

On Sackville River: Parsonage House of Revd. Mr. Gray *by John Elliott Woolford. The Reverend Benjamin Gerrish Gray was appointed to Sackville parish in 1806.*

Sackville Road runs along a ridge beside the Sackville River, and in the late 1750s, farm lots of five hundred acres were granted to would-be settlers along this road. The Fultz and Robinson families were among the earliest residents, with properties at the corner where the two roads diverged. There, William Fultz established an inn to serve travellers on both roads. Fultz's Inn was also known as the Twelve Mile House and served the public for many years, until it burned down in 1890. For travellers who made an early start out of Halifax, this was known to be a good place to stop for breakfast. Joseph Howe observed in his collected *Western and Eastern Rambles* that when travelling in 1829 it was "not so much a matter of course to get well fed at Fultz's, as to have a good appetite when you get there." The inn attracted not only travellers; for many years it was a destination for well-to-do residents of Halifax enjoying a day out of the city. The mile marker that once stood at what became known as Fultz's

Corner found a new home on the grounds of the nearby Fultz House Museum, established in the former home of Bennett Fultz, William's cousin.

Beyond Fultz's Inn, the string of houses that grew up along the road formed the nineteenth-century community of Sackville. A series of sketches and a map of the road drawn by John Elliott Woolford in 1817–1818 provide a clear picture of the community. Houses stood along both sides of the road for about thirteen kilometres, each with its area of cultivated land and wood lot that extended some distance back from the road. This was a community of farmers and loggers.

On a hill near the centre of the community, the original Anglican church of St. John the Evangelist was built around 1805. The first rector, the Reverend Benjamin Gerrish Gray, came to the parish in 1807. His parsonage house stood near the mouth of the Sackville River, but he also owned property and farmland not far from the church. The church burned one Sunday morning in 1828, just as the parishioners were assembling for the service. The building was replaced by the present church.

By 1818, Sackville had a school. Several inns served travellers on the Great Road to Windsor. This was the route for a stagecoach service initiated in February 1816 by Isaiah Smith. The coach carried mail, along with paying passengers and their baggage. The journey usually took about nine hours; frequent stops were necessary for refreshment and to change horses. The road was also used by private carriages, horsemen, and pedestrians. As well as the Ten Mile House and Fultz's Inn, the "houses of entertainment" along the road included Mitchell's Inn at Mile 14 (the distance at which coaches usually needed a change of horses) and Hamilton's Inn a mile further along.

In 1797, a small Black community led by James Palmer was established on land in what is now Middle Sackville formerly farmed by George F. Boyd and sold by his widow. The residents were Maroons from Jamaica—former rebels who had been deported to Halifax and settled in Preston. They had been converted to Christianity by the Reverend Gray and asked to be allowed to leave their discontented compatriots at Preston, in order to take up farming. The community, known as Boydville, was just beginning to succeed when an opportunity arose for the residents to leave with the other Maroons to start new lives in Sierra Leone. Palmer and his followers sailed out of Halifax Harbour in early August 1800. The name Maroon Hill survives as a reminder of their brief presence.

In the 1820s, Lieutenant-Governor Sir James Kempt embarked on a series of road improvements. One that came to his attention was the hilly route through Sackville. A new road was constructed to the east, running northward from Fultz's Corner. Known today as Sackville Drive, it became the main road to Windsor (now Trunk 1) replacing the old stagecoach route through Sackville. Likewise, the Old Cobequid Road gave way to Trunk 2. The opening of these roads marked the beginning of the expansion of the community, with more homes, inns, and other services. The roads would be superseded in their turn in the second half of the twentieth century by Highways 101 and 102.

By the end of the nineteenth century, Sackville's population had risen to over 850 people, the majority of whom were engaged in the farming or lumbering industries. As the population expanded, Upper, Middle, and Lower Sackville were recognized as distinct communities. A second church, Sackville United Baptist, was built in the 1830s, and a third, Knox Presbyterian, in 1890. From the mid-1850s, the Windsor branch of the Nova Scotia Railway provided an easy link from its Beaver Bank station to markets in Halifax for produce and lumber. Water-powered sawmills were operated by the Fenerty family and others, including the Heflers. The Fenertys ran a large business with several mills, but only the Hefler mill, which was said to be struggling for survival in the 1880s, has lasted to the present day. Under new ownership, it is now electrically operated in a new location visible from Highway 101.

After the Second World War, subdivisions grew up on former farmland, and for varying lengths of time, features such as the Sackville Drive-In Theatre, the Sackville Downs Raceway, and the Sackville Speedway entertained an increasingly suburban public. In the late 1960s, the provincial government encouraged the construction of housing for commuters who worked in Halifax and Dartmouth, and a much denser population developed. Bedford operated as a separate town from 1980 until 1996, when along with the Sackvilles, it was absorbed into Halifax Regional Municipality, where it now forms part of the greater Halifax area.

Today, Highway 101 has replaced Trunk 1 for most of the traffic from Halifax to Windsor, and Highway 102 carries the traffic to Truro and beyond. But if we take Trunk 1 at Lower Sackville and turn off by the Fultz House

Museum onto the Old Sackville Road, we find ourselves on a quiet route through the heart of the original settlement.

Mount Uniacke

Richard John Uniacke abandoned his articling with a Dublin attorney as a result of falling out with his father over religious differences. In 1774, he left home to seek his fortune across the Atlantic. After arriving in Philadelphia, he went into business with Moses Delesdernier, which took him to Nova Scotia. The following year Uniacke married Martha, the twelve-year-old daughter of his business partner, and his prospects were good. But in 1776, this adventurous young Irishman was marched unceremoniously along the Windsor Road, under arrest for his part in an uprising on the Chignecto Peninsula. He had unwisely supported a small American militia group in an attack on Fort Cumberland early in the Revolutionary War and was about to be tried for treason.

As he travelled along the Windsor Road with his captors, one of the places where the party paused for a rest reminded the prisoner of his family home in Ireland, which was called Mount Uniacke. It is said that he decided then and there to one day make his home at this spot. On his arrival in Halifax, the influence of some Irish military officers and some colonial government officials who were family friends spared him from being tried for treason. Leaving his pregnant wife in Nova Scotia, he returned to Ireland in 1777, completed his legal studies, and came back to Halifax in 1781.

The former rebel quickly became a respectable member of the colonial establishment. Uniacke was appointed Solicitor General and elected to the Assembly in 1783. His ambition was to become Nova Scotia's Attorney General, but his career faltered with the arrival, after the American Revolution, of powerful Loyalists who wanted the position to go to one of their own. Uniacke was passed over in favour of Sampson Salter Blowers. Nevertheless, he held various political positions, including the lucrative post of advocate general of the Vice-Admiralty Court, and eventually received the coveted appointment as Attorney General in 1797. He held this office until his death in 1830.

In 1784, Uniacke achieved the first step toward fulfilling his dream of becoming a country landowner by obtaining a grant of one thousand acres at the spot that had reminded him of his birthplace, midway between Halifax and Windsor. By the early nineteenth century, he had amassed a considerable fortune, enabling him to embark on the construction of a residence there. In 1815, he moved into his fine new home, a second Mount Uniacke, beside the lake that he named after his wife. Here he lived in semi-retirement, going to Halifax only when his duties as Attorney General required. He enjoyed the life of a country gentleman, entertaining guests from Halifax and well-to-do travellers along the Windsor Road. These included Lieutenant-Governor Dalhousie, who often stopped there on his way to or from Windsor and was sometimes an overnight guest. His lordship, in his journal, described the house as "the only Gentleman's seat on the road." Uniacke employed a fair number of servants in his household, as well as workers on the farm that he operated. They and their families formed the nucleus of the community that grew up around Mount Uniacke, from which it takes its name.

As one of the two great roads in Nova Scotia, the old road from Halifax to Windsor saw a good deal of traffic in the early nineteenth century. Settlers' homes grew up along the road, and some received subsidies from the government to offer hospitality to the travelling public. The population increased as people cleared readily accessible land for subsistence farms. In 1817, Lord Dalhousie described the habitations in his journal as "little Inns & cottages… very thickly set." The small farms and gardens produced enough for the residents' needs. In addition, they might have kept a cow, a pig, and a few chickens. By 1829, there was a blacksmith's shop on the edge of the Uniacke estate, serving the needs of both travellers and residents.

Uniacke was an enthusiastic supporter of Lord Dalhousie's efforts to persuade farmers to adopt up-to-date methods of agriculture. He had the land around his own house cleared and cultivated and brought in sheep and cattle. Instead of a fence to keep the livestock off his garden, he had a ha-ha built—a ditch with a vertical edge on the garden side, and invisible from the house so as not to interrupt the view. Although he experimented with scientific methods of farming, the poor soil was ill-suited for agriculture and the farm was never very productive. His neighbour and son-in-law, Collector of Customs Thomas Jeffrey, seems to have done rather better with his fine herd of cattle and his Scottish ploughman.

The employees in the Uniacke household must have had tales to tell when Lord Dalhousie returned to Nova Scotia in 1823 for a visit after his promotion to Governor General. He and his entourage were lavishly entertained at Mount Uniacke with a riotous reunion lasting three days. More than twenty guests, comprising the visitors and Halifax's leading citizens, enjoyed what must have been the greatest party in the community's history. Lord Dalhousie wrote in his journal that "all slept in the house, some even upon the billiard table, and Jeffray [sic] in the bathing house....In the evening Uniacke brought forward his Irish piper and all the servants & all the workmen and labourers assembled to dance."

The original stagecoach journey between Halifax and Windsor normally took nine hours, with stops every so often to change horses and pick up or drop off passengers, freight, and mail. In winter, sleighs replaced coaches and carriages. Travellers by private carriage and buggy made better time under normal conditions, but they also needed to stop every so often along the road for a meal and to change or rest their horses. Some farmers therefore became part-time innkeepers, offering rest, refreshment, and stabling. The Mount Uniacke community, midway between Halifax and Windsor, was a popular stopping point, and those travellers outside the Attorney General's social circle were often entertained at the nearby inn opened in 1802 by Jacob Pentz (or Pence) at his farm.

It was at the Pentz inn that Uniacke's son, Richard John Jr., took a room on the July day in 1819 when he killed William Bowie in Nova Scotia's last recorded fatal duel. It was an affair of honour fought with pistols: the two men had quarrelled when Uniacke implied in court that Bowie had been guilty of smuggling. After the first shots were exchanged neither man was hurt, and all would have ended well but Uniacke's second prevailed upon them to fire again, and this time Bowie was fatally wounded. Young Uniacke's status as the son of the Attorney General saved him from the gallows, as he was acquitted.

In 1858, the Nova Scotia Railway began to operate, offering an alternative mode of travel between Halifax and Windsor. A small depot was opened near the Pentz property at Mount Uniacke, which served until it was replaced by a new station in 1884. The area around the station quickly became the centre of the thriving community.

The most exciting time in the village's history was the period beginning in 1865, when David MacIntosh and John and Charles Sims discovered gold on the northern boundary of the Uniacke estate. Mining companies quickly moved in and staked claims in what became known as the Mount Uniacke Gold District. They constructed crushers to process the gold-bearing rock and built company houses for their employees. By the 1870s, there were hotels, stores, a tailor's shop, shoe shops, blacksmiths' and carpenters' shops, stables, a church, a meeting house, and a school at the site. A road ran up to the mines from Uniacke House, and another, now known as the Old Mines Road, was used by a wagon known as the "express" to carry passengers from the railway station. The company town was described in a newspaper in 1869 as looking "as if a running earthquake had just visited the spot, delving up all the rock and stone in its course, and nudging all the numerous houses together." But after the boom in the 1870s, gold production slowed as seams were depleted, and Mount Uniacke's mining community gradually declined. The last mine closed in 1941. Today nothing remains of the former company town, except for a few foundations deep in the forest. Some new homes have been built on the Old Mines Road, but the gold rush days are long gone.

Mount Uniacke remained a stopping place for travellers for many years, even as horse-drawn vehicles gave way to trains, and later, cars and trucks. While the gold mines were operating, the hotel beside the station served both mine employees and visitors. The last of several old hotels in the community was operated by Maynard Parker, who modernized an older building in 1925. It became a popular destination until it burned down in 1936. In the second half of the twentieth century, passenger train service was abandoned as improvements to the highway system resulted in a preference for travel by road, and Mount Uniacke station closed in 1963.

Uniacke House remained in the family until 1949, when it was acquired by the Nova Scotia government. It was opened in 1952 as part of the Nova Scotia Museum, which now operates the Uniacke Estate Museum Park. The old post road originally passed closer to Uniacke House than today's Trunk 1, which replaced it. A short section of the original road has survived as a walking trail in the park. The small community of Mount Uniacke has become a regional centre, with its school, library, post office, and other services. The entire area is now bypassed by Highway 101, but visitors to the museum site still drive along the former great road and contribute to the community's economy.

John Elliott Woolford's sketch, Mount Uniacke, *shows the house by the lake, and cleared farmland. The road has since been altered and no longer runs so close to the house.*

New Ross

In 1784, planning was initiated for a new direct road to link Halifax with Annapolis Royal, primarily for military purposes but also to encourage settlement. A line was surveyed between the two towns, and a trail was blazed. By 1786, work on the road had started, and a few lots were laid out for settlers at the western end; however, by the end of the eighteenth century, interest had faltered in developing the road as a military route. The project was revived in 1814 and John Harris was commissioned to survey a practical route for the road to follow. Road surveying and building resumed, and continued from 1816 to 1820, but construction at the eastern end proved too difficult because of the many lakes and rocky terrain. The project was abandoned, and the Halifax end of the road was never completed.

In 1816, the Government of Nova Scotia was looking for suitable land on which to settle soldiers who had been disbanded in the colony after taking part in the War of 1812. Some potential sites were surveyed along the Old

Annapolis Road. One of these was located on Gold River, an important route-way for the Mi'kmaq who called it Amapapskegek, or "Rocky River." Ancestral Indigenous campsites and places of cultural and spiritual significance lie along its banks. Today, the Gold River Reserve of the Acadia First Nation is located near the mouth of the river.

At the time when the settlement was laid out, according to Judge DesBrisay in his *History of the County of Lunenburg*, "Its only denizens were the moose, caribou, bear and other wild animals, and a few Micmac Indians, of whom the family of Penalls appeared to be the chief." This was Francis Pennell, or Parnell, who was born in Gold River in 1762, and lived there with his wife, Hannah Labrador, and their extended family.

Into this wilderness Captain William Ross led a group of 172 former soldiers from the Nova Scotia Fencibles, including some officers, along the rough trail that led northward up the Gold River from Chester Basin. The settlers' grant had been surveyed at a spot where the river widened into a lake, and where the trail met the Annapolis Road. Lots were laid out on the trail from Chester along the west side of the lake, and westward along the section now known as the Forties Road. Captain Ross was given a large lot overlooking the lake, where he brought his wife, Mary, and their children, Mary, William, Edward, and George. The new settlement was to be known as Sherbrooke, in honour of Lieutenant-Governor Sir John Coape Sherbrooke.

The settlers were issued rations for the initial period while they cleared their land, using the wood from trees they felled to build log cabins. The rations included beef, pork, and rum. While these lasted, all went well. But clearing the land and building homes proved daunting work, and when the rations were no longer supplied, many of the original grantees gave up and left. Those who remained survived by subsistence farming and by purchasing what supplies they could afford.

Life was hard at first. The community was extremely isolated, the expected road to Halifax remained unfinished, and the only access road was the rough trail from Chester Basin. Captain Ross did his best to encourage the settlers, setting an example by clearing land and building a log cabin for his family, which he later replaced with a frame house that he called Rosebank. The cottage is still standing. Another son, Lawson, was born to Captain and Mrs. Ross early in 1818, by which time they were well established.

That summer, Lord Dalhousie visited the community in the capacity of lieutenant-governor and described in his journal the access road as "scarcely passable for horses, about 12 miles…what with rocks & bogs& rotten trees I never hoped to accomplish the end without broken legs or arms." He survived the journey and found the Ross family living comfortably in their new home. He praised the efforts of the Rosses and other pioneers who had cleared their land and were doing well. He continued to take an interest in the community and the Ross family during his period of service in Nova Scotia. Before leaving, he presented young Mary with a piano, which some stalwart soldiers hauled up the trail from Chester, probably with much grumbling and cursing.

In the fall of 1821, hoping to further the establishment of the promised road to Halifax, William Ross set out with a Mi'kmaw guide, looking for a potential route through the inhospitable terrain. They were caught in a rainstorm and had to spend the night in the forest. Ross fell ill as a result of the experience, and never fully regained his health. He died the following spring, leaving Mary pregnant with another son, James, who was born in September. Her other children now ranged in age from four to fourteen, and the older ones helped her as best they could. Friends and neighbours also offered assistance, and somehow the family survived.

As the young Rosses grew up, they all pitched in to develop the property. Young Mary helped her mother run the busy household. She later married Andrew Kiens, the son of one of her father's fellow officers, and lived across the lake, often returning home for visits. We learn from a diary kept by Edward Ross that William, the eldest son, remained in the family home. He operated a sawmill and a gristmill, while his wife, Rachel, helped her mother-in-law with work around the house. George took charge of the farm, and made shoes in his spare time. As they became old enough, Lawson and James assisted wherever they were needed. Edward, who was educated at King's College School in Windsor, became an entrepreneur who ran a community store and marketed local produce as far away as Halifax. His business took him away from home from time to time, travelling by sea from Chester to the capital. Goods to stock his store were dragged up from the coast by oxen hauling a cart or a sled.

The men in the community worked in the fields and forests, while their spouses and daughters were busy about their houses. Everybody, particularly the women and younger boys, picked berries in season, and housewives made

"First piano owned in New Ross," photographed by Clara Dennis. This piano was given to young Mary Ross by Lord Dalhousie and carried by soldiers from Chester to Rosebank.

preserves for the winter months. Statute labour laws required householders to turn out with picks and shovels to maintain the roads when necessary, and the route from Chester gradually improved.

Life in New Ross, as it became known, was not all work. The family entertained at Rosebank Cottage with music, dancing, and a fair amount of drinking. Edward wrote in his diary about many merry parties there and at the homes of neighbours. While some of the Ross men eventually left, the property remained in the family until 1969, when the Ross Farm Museum was created.

New Ross expanded during the nineteenth century. In 1820, a school was established, with former naval officer James Wells appointed as schoolmaster. For many years, the nearest church was at Chester, and the first service in Sherbrooke, as it was known until 1863, was held by the Reverend Charles Inglis in the Ross home. The first Anglican church was built in about 1824 and was served by clergy from Chester. In 1854, the congregation of Christ Church welcomed its first resident priest. As the community grew, the original building was replaced by a larger one in 1879. A Roman Catholic chapel—the first in Lunenburg County—was built in 1827–28 and dedicated to St. Patrick. The present church replaced it in 1877. A small group of Baptists also came to the community, and elders were appointed in 1831; however, the first meeting house was not built until 1855–56.

The original Ross sawmill, built with handsaws and axes, was replaced by a new one in 1836. The first gristmill, which processed grain from the Ross farm and neighbouring fields, burned down and was rebuilt in 1838. A dam was built, and millstones installed, all without the mechanical equipment that would be used today. The sawmill produced lumber, a valuable source of income. Some of the wood was used at the Ross cooperage to produce barrels for sale in Halifax.

By the end of the century, the continuation of the trail from Chester Basin northward to Kentville that had been blazed in the early days of settlement had become a usable road. The Annapolis Road continued eastward as far as the road from Chester to Windsor, though it never reached Halifax. Homes were built along these roads, and the centre of the community grew up at the intersection, known for some obscure reason as Charing Cross, where a hotel and a blacksmith shop served the public.

The water-powered sawmill operated by William Ross and his brothers was only the beginning of the community's commercial development. By the 1880s, timber resources drove the economy of the area, and as many as fifty sawmills in the vicinity of New Ross were powered by its lakes and rivers. Today, forestry, with the added dimension of rejuvenating forests in a modern economy, and sawmilling are still important sources of income. As in most rural communities, businesses have diversified to serve both the residents and visitors.

The Ross Farm is now operated as a branch of the Nova Scotia Museum, giving visitors a glimpse of a working nineteenth-century farm, with a variety of animals, crops, a cooperage, a forge, and a collection of implements that were used before mechanization changed agricultural methods. Local people in costume replicate work on the farm as the Ross family knew it. In Rosebank Cottage, women tend the wood stove and bake cookies for visitors. A one-room school, typical of its day, has been moved to the grounds. A walk around the fields, visits to the buildings, and a ride in the horse-drawn wagon or sleigh transport us back to the early days of life in New Ross.

The Wentworth Valley Communities

The Cobequid Mountains have always created a formidable barrier between the main part of Nova Scotia to the south and the land to the north toward the Chignecto Isthmus. Over the years, travellers have favoured different routes over the mountains from Halifax to Amherst and beyond to New Brunswick. In the early 1800s, it was usual to travel by water across the Minas Basin to Parrsboro and then northward by a road along Farrells River and River Hébert, or to take the road from Truro through Onslow and Londonderry, and over the Westchester Mountain to Amherst. And for many years in the twentieth century, the main provincial highway, Trunk 4, ran westward from Onslow and then turned northward at Glenholme to continue through the valley of the Folly River and over Folly Mountain, before descending between the steep slopes of the Wentworth Valley.

Today, Highway 104 bypasses the valley, running more or less directly northwestward from Truro by way of the Cobequid Pass across Westchester Mountain. Trunk 4 still offers an alternative route, now free of most commercial traffic, through the scenic Wentworth Valley and along the Wallace River, passing through spots identified on the map as Wentworth Valley, Wentworth, Wentworth Centre, and West Wentworth, with Lower Wentworth on Route 307 branching north toward the Northumberland Shore. These, with Wentworth Station on the western slope, form the scattered and sparsely populated communities that took their name from Sir John Wentworth, who came to Nova Scotia in 1783 as surveyor general of the King's woods and served as lieutenant-governor from 1792 to 1808.

The first settlers came to the Wentworth Valley in the 1770s. They cleared land along the Wallace River. They obtained grants and established farms. The first grant of nine hundred acres on the river went to two men named Tuttle and Allen. The Herley family farmed the first cleared land at Lower Wentworth. Early residents included a young couple named Miers who were said to have walked all the way from Massachusetts, and the young members of the McKand family who came from Scotland with only their mother, their father having decided at the last minute to remain behind. Mrs. McKand came anyway and raised her family in a log cabin at West Wentworth. Log cabins were also the first residences of her neighbours until sawmills were established.

The railway runs through the Wentworth Valley, with a view over farmland to the wooded hills beyond.

While the valley's soil supported some farming, logging played the major role in Wentworth's economy from early days. The area was thickly forested, and logs were processed by the water-powered sawmills that were soon constructed on the brooks along the Wallace River; some of them also functioned as gristmills. Once sawn lumber was available, the settlers gradually replaced the early log cabins with frame houses. The first of these houses was built by Secord Beebe on the Westchester Road. It had twenty-five centimetre–thick wooden walls, designed to be bullet-proof in the days when settlers still feared raids by the Mi'kmaq. Like the rest of Nova Scotia, this was Indigenous territory, and the settlers were well aware they were regarded as intruders.

High up the valley, Washington Hart operated a sawmill on the brook that bears his name. Others were Rufus Purdy's mill on Whetstone Brook, William Drennen's and the Ogilvie brothers' mills on what is now Mahoney Brook, and Cornelius Crowley's on Crowley Brook. The Wallace River powered Amos Purdy's sawmill, as well as the Maclean brothers' sawmill, gristmill, and carding mill, among many others along the river. The sawn lumber was formed into rafts and floated downriver, either towed by a boat or guided with poles handled by men riding on the rafts, to be shipped to various destinations from Wallace Harbour.

Other businesses grew up along the Wallace River. There were stores in each of the small communities that developed. Lower Wentworth also had a blacksmith shop, a carriage shop, a tannery, and shoemaker's shop. There was another blacksmith shop at Wentworth, and there were two at West Wentworth. The owner of one of these, Robert Henderson, also made butter tubs. The area's economy was based on its vast supply of lumber, but hope was raised for the development of another resource with the discovery of copper at the end of the nineteenth century in the northern part of the community. The Feeley Mine was established at Lower Wentworth and the Palmer Mine at West Wentworth. The copper-bearing rocks were hauled by wagon to a smelter at Wentworth Centre, established in 1901 by William Hogan and his father. The small settlement looked set to become an industrial community. The smelter provided work for about a dozen men who were housed along with the mine workers at the Crown Copper Hotel at Wentworth. But the copper business was not successful; it closed in 1904, leaving workers unpaid. The hotel building became a store, which was still standing in the 1960s.

The Intercolonial Railway line was built in the late nineteenth century to connect Halifax with Central Canada. The section through the Wentworth Valley was opened in 1872. The major engineering project involved moving huge quantities of rock to level the roadbed. The tracks ran along the mountain on the west side of the river, offering a spectacular view across the valley. The scenery was described in the *Halifax Morning Chronicle* in October 1872 as "a scene of grandeur and beauty unequalled by any other on the line."

Wentworth Station stands a little to the west of the highway, where the line turns toward Oxford. The opening of the railway enabled lumber to be sent to market and goods to be brought from the capital by rail instead of by sea, and travellers could make an easier journey to other parts of the province and beyond. The station had freight and lumber sheds, and there were stores, hotels, livery stables, and a carriage shop in the community. Before a rail line was developed from Oxford to Pictou, a stagecoach met the train at Wallace Station and carried passengers to Wallace and the Northumberland Shore. In 1903, a one-room schoolhouse was built at Wentworth Station—one of six schools serving the Wentworth area.

Sawmilling and woodworking continued in the Wentworth Valley into the early twentieth century, when the Rhodes Curry Company of Amherst opened a sawmill that put the smaller mills out of business. For a few years, from about 1917, William Swan operated his Maritime Handle Factory, but it was burned out twice. After the second fire in the early 1920s, it did not reopen.

Heavy snow is common in the Wentworth Valley area. In the early days of settlement, when the road through the Wentworth Valley was impassible in winter, residents were dependent on the railway for access to the southern part of the province. But the snow also opened up possibilities: after the Second World War, the first attempt was made to create a ski resort in the Wentworth Valley. A succession of mild winters caused the venture to be abandoned. The idea was revived in the 1950s, and the first ski tow was installed in 1956. The 1960s saw the improvement of the road as part of the Trans-Canada Highway, which became the main route to the province's border with New Brunswick and thus was more regularly cleared in winter months. With improved access, development naturally followed. A combined ski lodge and youth hostel was built, and a T-bar ski lift was installed in the 1960s. Facilities have been improved over the years. A good snow season now brings many visitors to the area, while in summer, they can enjoy hiking and biking on the trails.

In 1958, the small schools closed that served the individual communities. The younger students went by bus to the new Consolidated Elementary School at Wentworth Centre, while grades seven and upward transferred to Pugwash District High School.

By the second half of the twentieth century, logs and other goods were transported increasingly by truck, and private cars became many people's preferred method of travel. The narrow highway was heavily used, and lumber trucks and other commercial traffic crawled slowly up Folly Mountain, frustrating car drivers trying to reach the Wentworth Valley. Relief came in 1997, with the opening of Highway 104 through the Cobequid Pass, which provided a faster route.

Today, the small sawmills on the river have long since closed and much of the farmland is abandoned. Wood is still harvested, and lumber is marketed through the North Nova Forest Owners Co-op at Wentworth Centre. Skiers, snowboarders, and hikers make good use of Ski Wentworth trails in season, contributing to the economy. After the elementary school closed,

Wentworth Centre's Learning Centre took over the former school building and now serves as a hub for community activities. Today, many residents work elsewhere. Travellers on the now quiet Trunk 4 over Folly Mountain can still enjoy the peaceful scenery of the Wentworth Valley.

RAILWAY TOWNS

A network of railways was constructed in the province in the second half of the nineteenth century. These provided faster transportation for heavy goods and farm produce and offered passengers a quicker and more comfortable alternative to road travel. When the Nova Scotia Railway opened in the late 1850s, it was the beginning of a network of train tracks operated by different companies that eventually extended throughout the province. Trains and tracks required maintenance, stations had to be staffed, and railway workers formed a high proportion of towns' populations. Communities expanded around junctions and important stations, where warehouses were built to store goods for transport. The places where these lines came together were already established communities, but they became important transfer points for both goods and passengers, and their economies grew as a result. The prosperity brought by the railways began to drop off as private cars and trucks took over much of their traffic. One by one, the rail lines closed down, so that by the twenty-first century only the main lines to central Canada and Cape Breton were operating. Former railway towns have had to diversify, and some stations have been lost or repurposed. Disused tracks were taken up and their routes converted to recreational trails.

Bridgewater

By the end of the nineteenth century and for much of the twentieth, Bridgewater was an important railway town. But its history goes back far beyond the establishment of railways. For thousands of years, the spot at the tidehead on the LaHave River where the town now stands was a well-used Indigenous inland encampment. The Mi'kmaq knew the river well, and called it Pijinuiskaq, meaning "river of long joints." Artifacts dating back thousands of years were discovered on the riverbanks near the town. Birchbark canoes could still be seen on the river for many years after the town was established, although it was increasingly difficult for the Mi'kmaw inhabitants to maintain their traditional way of life. Judge DesBrisay of Bridgewater, who built a collection of Mi'kmaw artifacts, was sympathetic to the challenges the Indigenous people faced and expressed his disapproval of the imperial attitude toward them. He wrote in his *History of the County of Lunenburg*, published in 1895, "The Micmacs are a much neglected people. While the benefits they derive from the civilization around them are small, their hunting-grounds have been destroyed, which has deprived them of the means of living enjoyed by their forefathers, and they have been made familiar with the vices to which they were formerly strangers. They are furnished, as if by way of acknowledging their changed situation, with a few blankets in winter, and in time of great scarcity, with some additional provisions. We would fain see more done to place them above want and make their lives happy."

In 1765, Joseph Pernette received a huge land grant on the west side of the LaHave River stretching from the falls above the present town of Bridgewater as far as LaHave. He established his homestead at West LaHave, which became the centre of settlement for the rest of the eighteenth century. It was only in the nineteenth century that settlers moved upriver. The first houses in what is now Bridgewater were built on the west side before 1815 by Ralph Hotchkiss, a shoemaker, and by Garret and Frederick Wile, who ran a sawmill at the mouth of what is now Wiles Brook. Others followed on both sides of the river. Residents relied upon a ferry run by James Nicholson to travel from one side of the LaHave to the other.

For many years, travellers on the post road from Lunenburg to Liverpool and beyond had crossed the river by a ferry at West LaHave operated by John Pernette. By the 1820s, there was sufficient traffic that the post road was re-routed between Mahone Bay and Liverpool by way of a bridge over the LaHave at the head of tide. In 1825, the bridge was constructed a short distance upriver from the present-day bridges. It was built on log piers, with wooden planking, and it is said that thirteen 100-gallon barrels of rum were consumed during its construction. Once it was built, Bridgewater rapidly became the commercial centre for the surrounding region.

For many years, James Starratt ran a hotel on the west side of the river, where businesses quickly grew up along the main street. In 1848, young Robert

Dawson came to Bridgewater to run the town's first store on behalf of Halifax merchant Joseph Jennings. After a short time, the young man bought out his employer and developed one of Bridgewater's major businesses, operating not only a retail hardware store in a building that still stands but also trading ships that carried lumber and locally produced goods for export. Among other prominent Bridgewater businessmen in early days were merchants John Hebb, Joseph Miller, James Grinton, Joseph Whitford, Robert West, and Samuel Ramey, and shipbuilder Andrew Gow. Goods were brought in or exported by the vessels moored at the line of wharves along the LaHave River. Captain Joseph Wade was appointed the port's shipping master and collector of customs.

In the second half of the nineteenth century, as well as the businesses established along the main street, a series of industries grew up on Wiles Brook, which runs into the LaHave River at the north end of town. High up on the brook stood a water-powered gristmill, operated first by Robert Whitman and later by his son. A little lower down, near the junction of High Street and Victoria Road, the brook provided power for Waterman's tannery. James Edward Waterman, his brother Joseph, and his cousin Thomas ran the tannery and a shoemaking business under the name J. E. Waterman & Co., until the company went into bankruptcy the 1920s. It was later revived and maintained by John L. Waterman until 1955. The third operation on the brook was a carding mill, established in 1860 by Dean Wile, who gave his name to the brook. Thomas Waterman and Duncan Macmillan opened the Bridgewater Foundry, near the carding mill, in 1864. It changed hands several times before closing in the early twentieth century. At the foot of the brook stood a carriage shop generally known as the wagon factory, operated by William and James Veinot, with an adjoining blacksmith shop. Of all the businesses on the brook, only the carding mill survives, now operated as part of the Nova Scotia Museum.

Bridgewater's central industry for many years was sawmilling. Lumber, a major export, was carried to distant ports as well as to destinations in Canada, by the large sailing ships, some locally built, that lined Bridgewater's wharves. Much of this lumber was rafted downriver from two mills, just above the town, that Edward Doran Davison bought in 1865. These were known as the upper and lower mills. Davison came with his family to Bridgewater from Mill Village, where he had gained experience as a lumber dealer. His sons joined him in the business, and for many years, E. D. Davison & Sons was the leading employer in the growing town. By the end of the 1880s, the company had expanded to include a total of five mills on the LaHave, Medway, and Nictaux Rivers, with its headquarters in Bridgewater. Davison's was at that time the largest lumber business in Nova Scotia, and he became known as the province's Lumber King. The company was sold in 1903 to John Hastings of Pittsburgh and continued to be a driving force in the town's economy, until declining demand for lumber brought about its closure in 1921.

Bridgewater's history as a railway town began in 1889, when the Nova Scotia Central Railway opened, running from Middleton to Bridgewater and continuing to Mahone Bay and Lunenburg. The line was purchased in 1902 by the Halifax and Southwestern Railway, which was building a line from the capital to Yarmouth. The company made its headquarters where the lines met in Bridgewater. A railway bridge just above the town carried the trains across the river. Goods varying from barrels of apples to lumber, once shipped by water from wharves along the river, were now brought to the railway station by ox carts and horse-drawn wagons. In 1918, the line became part of the Canadian National Railway system, linking Bridgewater to the rest of Canada. When the Davison mills closed, the blow was cushioned as the railway provided employment for many of Bridgewater's residents. Another major employer was the Acadia Gas Engines Company, known for its "make and break" fishing boat engines, which operated from 1908 until the 1970s.

Bridgewater suffered a setback in 1899, when fire broke out in the basement of the music hall on the main street and spread quickly, destroying fifty-four of the buildings in the town's centre. But rebuilding started immediately, and the town was incorporated later that same year. At the end of the nineteenth century, there was intense rivalry between Bridgewater and Lunenburg as to which should be the administrative centre of the province. Lunenburg was older and home to an important fishing fleet. Bridgewater was a busy industrial town. Both towns had courthouses: Lunenburg's was built in 1892, Bridgewater's the following year. After much controversy, it was decided that the honour should be shared, with the spring sitting held in Lunenburg and the fall sitting in Bridgewater.

Bridgewater's station was the hub of the town's activities in the early twentieth century.

Bridgewater remained a busy railway town for many years, with much of its economy centred on its fine station, its shunting yard, and its roundhouse. In the 1950s, days were still punctuated by the sound of locomotives blowing their horns as they approached the town, where they had to cross what was then the main road from Halifax, holding up traffic. They sounded day and night as freight trains were broken up and the cars assembled in the shunting yard, crossing the highway each time they moved back and forth. Both passenger and freight traffic dropped off in the second half of the century. Passenger service ended in 1969, and the station closed. It was destroyed by a mysterious fire in 1982, and the site is now occupied by the East Side shopping mall. By 1993, freight service had been abandoned, the line was closed, and the town became unusually quiet. Lunenburg's Railway Museum has an interesting diorama recreating the busy station with model trains coming and going.

Other changes came about in the second half of the twentieth century. Shopping malls replaced the main street as the chief retail centres, and chain stores replaced many independent businesses. The focus of the town's economy shifted, and the population increased again as the Michelin tire company opened a plant at the north end of the town, where a business park also grew up. New retail businesses have come to Bridgewater, which has become the largest town of the South Shore and its commercial centre. Its amenities include parks, a recreation centre, and a multi-use trail replacing the former railway track. The DesBrisay Museum, based on the judge's original collection of historic artifacts, displays items ranging from the earliest days of the town's history to more recent times.

Middleton, Annapolis County

Nova Scotia has three Middletons: one "in the middle" between Tatamagouche and River John; one seemingly in the middle of nowhere in Antigonish County; and the largest halfway along the Annapolis Valley, which is of course why it got its name. Also known as "the Heart of the Valley," Middleton lies on the north bank of the Annapolis River, at the point where the Nictaux River flows into it from lakes in the province's interior. The Annapolis River was a major routeway for the Mi'kmaq, who fished for shad at the confluence of the rivers in the area that they called Niktaq, meaning "the forks of a river."

In the seventeenth century, the river valley provided an inland link between Acadian communities at Port Royal, on the lower part of the rivière du Dauphin (the Annapolis River), and those around the Minas Basin. The Acadians certainly travelled through the area that is now Middleton, though there is no record of Acadian villages anywhere on the river above Bridgetown.

British colonization began only after the deportation, with the arrival of the Planters who came to Wilmot Township from New England in the 1760s. The area that would become Middleton was part of this township, and grants along the river there were surveyed for the Gates, Marshall, Richardson, and Neily families. Their land was laid out in long strips extending from the river to the North Mountain, allowing for both farming and logging as well as providing access to the river. The pioneer families were joined in the 1780s by a group of Loyalists, and the township's population increased.

The Reverend John Wiswall also came to the area in the 1780s, under the auspices of the Society for the Propagation of the Gospel. With the encouragement of Bishop Charles Inglis, he oversaw and took part in the building of the Church of Holy Trinity to serve the parish of Wilmot. The building was begun in 1789, in what is now Lower Middleton, on a piece of land provided by Governor Parr for the church and burial ground. The first service was conducted in 1791 by Bishop Inglis in the then-incomplete building. Work on the interior and the steeple continued, and construction was completed six years later. The church is still standing today. John Wiswall became the first rector and served the parish until his death in 1812.

By 1792, a post road had been established along the Annapolis Valley, running along the north side of the Annapolis River. At first it was little more than a trail, used initially by a courier on horseback to carry mail from Halifax to Annapolis and Digby. By 1818, it had been improved sufficiently that the Western Stage Coach service ran three times a week between Halifax and Annapolis, collecting and delivering mail and picking up and dropping passengers along the way.

In the early nineteenth century, the centre of population shifted eastward from Lower Middleton to the site of today's town, at what was known as Wilmot Corner or Fowler's Corner. Here, the main road along the Valley intersected with roads running north to the Bay of Fundy and south along the Nictaux River toward Bridgewater. One of the handful of houses at the crossroads served as an inn. The community was also called Gates Ferry, recalling the ferry across the Annapolis River that was run by the Gates family before a bridge was built. At a town meeting in 1854, it was decided to rename the community Middleton because of its location halfway along the Valley, and midway between Halifax and Yarmouth.

As communications improved, the community expanded. Its location at the crossroads encouraged the development of businesses in the town, which served as the market centre for the surrounding agricultural district. The Pearce Hotel was a welcome stopping place on the stagecoach route. The construction of the Windsor and Annapolis Railway began in 1866, and the line was opened in 1869, stimulating more activity in the town. A train station was constructed at Middleton, where farmers brought their produce, in carts drawn by oxen decorated with jingling bells, for transport to market in Halifax. Two more hotels, Hatfield House and American House, were opened, and Middleton offered food and lodging to both travellers and residents of the surrounding area who came to town on business.

Middleton's historic train station is now one of the town's museums.

In 1891, the Nova Scotia Central Railway opened a line linking Middleton with Bridgewater and Lunenburg, and the following year a new station building was erected to accommodate the increasing traffic. Middleton Station, at the junction of the two lines, was becoming a busy place, handling transshipments of goods from both the Valley and the South Shore. Passengers changed from one line to another, and freight trains were disassembled and rail cars switched to their destinations. All this activity provided employment for Middleton residents. By the end of the century, the town had schools and two new churches—one Anglican and the other Baptist. With the population expanding, there was a bank and a telephone service. A town reservoir ensured a constant water supply.

The twentieth century ushered in further innovations. The wooden Armoury building, associated with the D Company of West Nova Scotia Regiment, was constructed in 1902 for the community's militia. It was followed the next year by the Macdonald Consolidated School, the first of its kind in Canada. Sir William C. Macdonald, a prosperous tobacco merchant and educational philanthropist, founded several such schools in rural areas, bringing together the children from smaller schools to provide them with a good education. A small hospital set up in a house in Lower Middleton opened in 1916. It was relocated several times before the Soldiers Memorial Hospital was opened in 1921 in a larger building on Middleton's Commercial Street. The present Soldiers Memorial Hospital was built in 1961.

In the early 1900s, a third railway came to Middleton. The Victoria Beach Railway was constructed to carry iron ore mined at Torbrook, south of the town, to Port Wade for export. The Torbrook mine closed in 1913, making the railway redundant. Meanwhile, the Windsor and Annapolis Railway had become part of the Dominion Atlantic Railway, and the Nova Scotia Central Railway had been taken over by the Halifax and Southwestern. Middleton's role as a hub of rail transport contributed considerably to its prosperity. The town was at the centre of a flourishing apple-growing region, and every autumn barrels of apples were shipped by train to Halifax. In 1915, the train station was replaced once again by the building that stands today.

The early twentieth century also saw the establishment of new businesses. In 1901, a mill and woodworking shop were opened by Amos William Allen and his son, Joe. They produced all kinds of millwork, cabinetry, and institutional and home furnishings and quickly gained province-wide recognition for fine-quality work. In spite of two serious fires, in 1939 and 1945 respectively, Allen's mill is still in business today. In 1903, George Reagh founded the family business of G. N. Reagh and Sons, manufacturing cream separators, barrels, and farm implements and employing twenty-five workers. The company was known in 1925 as Reagh's Cooperage. It remained a family business for many years, later merging to become part of Tingley, Reagh, and Adams, a wholesale grocery company, which transferred operations from Middleton to other parts of Atlantic Canada.

In 1923, J. D. McKenzie established the McKenzie Creamery in a former hotel building. It remained in the family until 1977, when it was taken over by Twin City Dairies. The Scotian Gold canning factory processed fruit and vegetables from Valley farms from 1935 until the late 1950s, when it was bought out and closed. Apples have given way to more diverse produce in the region.

The railways remained busy until after the Second World War, when roads began to replace rails as the principal means of commercial and passenger transport. The line to Bridgewater was closed in 1982 and the Dominion Atlantic Railway ceased operations in 1994. But Middleton's historical importance as a railway town has not been forgotten. The former station building now houses the Middleton Railway Museum, with its impressive locomotive and its collection of railway memorabilia. The old railway lines have been given new life as popular cycling and hiking trails.

Other attractions bring visitors to Middleton: the former Macdonald Consolidated School building has also been converted into a museum, with exhibits depicting the early life of the town, including a reconstructed classroom and general store, and a natural history exhibit. It houses the Nova Scotia collection of antique clocks and watches. Another interesting clock stands outside the Town Hall. It is operated by water, using a technique developed by the Babylonians dating back to 1400 BC.

Old Holy Trinity Church in Lower Middleton has stood virtually unaltered since it was built by the Loyalists in the late eighteenth century. A simple wooden building with large rectangular windows and a balcony, it retains its original pews and pulpit, and has been designated as a Nova Scotia Heritage Site. No longer the main parish church, it is used for special services and events, and is open to visitors in summer. Many of Middleton's early settlers lie in its graveyard. A second recognized heritage building is the Middleton Armoury, built on the town's main street.

The centre of Middleton remains the meeting place of important roads. Here, Trunk 10, the road from Bridgewater and New Germany, meets Trunk 1, formerly the main road through the Annapolis Valley. Today, visitors also arrive by Highway 101, which bypasses the town to the north. In the twenty-first century, the town's businesses have diversified, but the hospitality industry still welcomes visitors.

Truro

Truro is known as "the Hub of Nova Scotia," which is apt as it lies approximately at the centre of mainland Nova Scotia. Maps show lines that represent the province's highways and railways radiating out like the spokes of a wheel, but this was a communications centre long before European settlement. The Salmon River, which the Mi'kmaq called Plamui-sipu, and the North River (Matawipukwejk, meaning "river of the fork") meet here, while McClures Brook (Niktuipukwek, "flowing forkwise") comes in from the south. These waterways formed a crossroad from the north, south, east, and west. They allowed the Mi'kmaq to travel easily for great distances around Mi'kma'ki between summer and winter quarters and to meet and trade at this traditional encampment. The area around the mouth of the river was known as We'kobetkitk ("end of flow"), from which the name Cobequid is derived. The area south of Truro is now the home of the Millbrook First Nation, or Niktuipukwek.

Most Acadians had been living in Port Royal before a group of them began to move to the marshlands around Cobequid Bay. In 1689, Mathieu Martin, a weaver by trade, was granted land on the bay, along with the title of seigneur of Cobequid, in recognition of his being the first French child to be born in Acadie. His parents, Pierre Martin and Catherine Vigneau, had come to LaHave in 1636, and moved to Port Royal. Matthieu Martin was unable to take possession of his grant immediately, as the title of seigneur was disputed by an official at Port Royal, Mathieu de Goutin. Only when the matter was resolved was Martin able to develop his property.

In 1699, the first Acadian families, relatives of Mathieu Martin, came from Port Royal and Grand Pré to the Seigneurie de Saint Martin. They were Germain Therriot, who was married to Martin's niece, Anne Pellerin; Pierre Therriot, Germain's brother; Martin Bourg, a brother-in-law to Martin's sister; and Martin Blanchard and his nephew Jérôme Guérin. Others soon followed. They built dykes and aboiteaux around the bay and along the river, planted crops, and raised sheep, cattle, and hogs. By 1714, there were twenty-three families at Cobequid. Except for those living in the small community of Vil Bois Brûlé near today's downtown Truro, they were scattered widely over the extensive seigneurie. The population had risen to about eight hundred by 1748.

The Acadian residents were on good terms with the Mi'kmaq inhabitants, who continued to use their long-established travel routes and their encampment at the mouth of the Salmon River. Mathieu Martin died some time before 1724, and despite claims by his heirs, his seigneurial land passed to the British Crown. Most Acadians had already left the area for the neighbouring French colonies before 1755; any who remained were deported and their homes were burned to discourage their return.

Their departure left their farms abandoned. Responding to Governor Lawrence's invitation to New Englanders to take up land in Nova Scotia, people of Scots-Irish descent from New Hampshire came to settle here in 1761. The new arrivals sailed into the mouth of the Salmon River, where the town of Truro was laid out for them. It consisted of house lots, school and church lots, a burial ground and a parade square. The settlers began building their houses and reviving the township's derelict farmland.

In 1768, a meeting house was erected and remained in use until 1854, when a new Presbyterian church replaced it. The first school opened in about 1775, followed by a grammar school in 1800. Truro's population increased in the 1780s with the arrival of Loyalists from the United States, including a significant number of Black Loyalists. The grants in rural Truro Township included woodlots as well as farmland, and lumbering was an important source of income. By the end of the 1780s, the relatively bustling community called Truro had four water-powered sawmills and a shipyard.

Late eighteenth-century maps already show "roads" radiating from Truro to Halifax, to Tatamagouche, Pictou, and beyond, and to Fort Cumberland; however, they were not necessarily fit for wheeled vehicles. When James MacGregor travelled by land from Halifax to Pictou in 1786, he found the route to Truro was a rough and rocky trail, mostly through dense forest. The journey on horseback took nearly three days. The trail to Pictou was worse. Ten years later, parts of the route were still nothing but a blazed trail. But by 1816, the Cobequid Road was passable enough to allow for the establishment of a stagecoach service between the capital and Truro, with just one overnight stop along the way. The service was soon extended to Pictou, and wheeled traffic increased as the radiating trails became roads, though these roads remained unpaved until the twentieth century.

The nineteenth century was a period of swift development in Truro. As the centre of an agricultural area, Truro became the site of a cattle show, which is still an annual event. When Lord Dalhousie attended it in 1819, it was in its infancy. Nevertheless, he remarked in his journal that the event attracted "a great concourse of people and a more numerous exhibition of cattle than I saw in Horton—they were also in better condition. Some excellent pigs imported this year from England. Sheep very wretched. A good Bull of the Ayrshire breed…but none of the cows good." He remained optimistic for future improvements.

In 1829, Joseph Howe travelled by stagecoach from Halifax to Truro, which, he observed, arrived late. He stayed at the Blanchard home on "The Hill" (now Bible Hill) on the north bank of the river. In his collected writings *Western and Eastern Rambles*, he described this area as having "tasty [sic] and neatly built houses scattered over this division of the village." On the south side was the "collection of buildings that make up the little town. The Episcopal Church is the most prominent object, and around and beyond it are scattered some sixty or seventy houses, of various sizes and structure, to the most of which are connected small fields and gardens—some enclosed very tastefully by little white rails." The town's mills stood "at the lower extremity of a small lake—Grist, Fulling, Saw, and Oat Mill." The lake and falls that powered these mills are now part of Victoria Park.

Truro was clearly prospering. The first post office was built in 1836. In 1841, the Colchester Academy replaced the former grammar school. The original courthouse was replaced by a new building in 1844. The Provincial Normal School opened in 1855 to train the province's teachers. Two years later, the academy was replaced by a Model School, where student teachers could practise. In 1885, the School of Agriculture opened. Education remains important in Truro. The Normal School became the Nova Scotia Teachers College and moved to a new building in 1961. It closed in 1997, and the building now serves as the Colchester County Museum. Truro's schools have become the Chignecto Central Regional Centre for Education, serving students from a wide area. In 1905, the Nova Scotia Agricultural College was established at Bible Hill, replacing the School of Agriculture; in 2012 it became the Agricultural Campus of Dalhousie University.

From the late 1850s, students at the Provincial Normal School practised their teaching skills at this Model School.

Truro's days as a railway town began in 1858, when the Nova Scotia Railway line from Halifax to Truro opened, with a continuation to Pictou that later became part of the main line to Cape Breton. The Nova Scotia Railway became part of the Intercolonial system, and 1873 saw the opening of the Intercolonial line from Truro to Amherst, with a roundhouse and a new station in Truro that employed many workers. The line would later extend to Quebec and Montreal. Truro's importance as a railway junction increased when the Midland Railway from Truro to Windsor opened in 1901, adding another spoke to the hub, and contributing further to the town's economy. A fourth spoke followed with the opening of a line to Cape Breton. The railways made accessible a market for local produce that could be shipped rapidly to various destinations, and the station was an important transshipment point for all kinds of freight. Station staff, train crews, and maintenance workers formed an important part of Truro's population.

Better communications brought industrial expansion. Sawmilling had always been an important industry, and in the second half of the century, steam was replacing water as the mills' source of power. According to Barbara Robertson's *Sawpower*, the Excelsior Steam mill produced three million board feet of lumber annually in the late 1870s. A few years later, Thomas G. McMullen operated three steam mills and one still powered by water. Truro Iron Foundry was established in 1863, producing stoves, ship and mill castings, heaters, and tinware. In the 1880s, it became the Truro Foundry and Machine Company, with ten buildings and forty-two employees. Robertson notes in *Sawpower* that the business was engaged in manufacturing "stoves, boilers, iron bridges, piano plates, shafting, ploughs, tinware, rotary sawmills, shingle mills, and steam engines."

An offshoot of Nova Scotia's lumber industry was the proliferation of woodworking factories in the late nineteenth century, as prosperous business-men built themselves substantial homes. The Truro Sash and Door Factory opened in 1884. It produced more than its name would indicate: by the 1890s the factory was making mouldings, brackets, counters, school desks, and build-ing materials—all in demand both in the growing community and in other parts of the province. Other businesses using wood ranged from the Truro Furniture Manufacturing Company to the Truro Last & Peg Factory, which manufactured clothespins exported by the barrel.

In 1870, Charles Stanfield founded the Truro Woolen Mills, later renamed the Stanfield Mill. A larger factory replaced the original one in 1882, produc-ing a range of yarns and clothing. Stanfield sold the business to his sons in 1896, and they developed a process to prevent their garments from shrinking; the iconic drop-seated "unshrinkables" became bestsellers. Stanfield's became known as the chief source of men's underwear across Canada.

The twentieth and twenty-first centuries have unfolded with many changes. The old steam sawmills and the woodworking factories have closed; today, J. D. Irving's Truro sawmill is located a short distance upriver from the town. Stanfield's is the only survivor of Truro's original large manufacturing busi-nesses. The Crossley Carpet factory opened in 1964, and employed over two hundred workers, but its operations were recently moved to the United States. Truro remains the home of many small businesses.

Today, the main Canadian National Railway line to Montreal still runs through Truro, though passenger service is much diminished. A line no longer runs to Windsor, and the future of the remaining freight line to Cape Breton is uncertain. Unlike Bridgewater and Middleton, Truro still has a working train station, but its importance as a railway town has declined. It remains a communications hub; roads radiate from the town, and the 102 and 104 Highways link it to the capital and to distant parts of the province. Now, the journey from Halifax that took James MacGregor nearly three days takes only an hour.

Stanfield Mills from Salmon River Bridge, Truro, Nova Scotia.

4

INDUSTRIAL COMMUNITIES

While coastal communities grew up around the industries of fish processing and shipbuilding, people who moved inland depended on industries arising from the land and the forest for their living. New settlers had to carve their homes from often dense forest and break up the soil to grow their food. Other supplies had to be bought, and the sale of lumber and surplus produce from their farms became their chief source of income. Sawmills and gristmills were their first mechanized businesses. Mineral extraction also evolved in inland areas, where communities quickly sprang up. Specialized trades such as carpentry and blacksmithing were needed, and tanneries, carding mills, and foundries were established. These formed the foundations of the industries of our inland communities.

Some of these people brought their skills to Nova Scotia after the American Revolution, when Alexander McNutt brought Scots-Irish immigrants from New Hampshire to populate the new township of Londonderry between Cobequid Bay and the Cobequid Mountains. They were joined a few years later by another Scots-Irish group from Ulster. The Scottish settlers around the New Glasgow area were instrumental in establishing industries there. Cornish and Welsh miners came to extract the province's mineral resources.

Lumbering, preparing trees for sale, is one of Nova Scotia's oldest industries. As communities were established, sawmills were built on nearby brooks to alleviate much hard manual labour. Lumber was not only used locally but also sold to nearby shipyards and exported all over the world. In some communities, milling quickly became the chief driver of the economy. The prosperity of other communities was based on mining and manufacturing, as raw materials were found and processed into finished goods ranging from heavy machinery to textiles made from locally produced wool. In the late nineteenth century, these industries brought prosperity to many communities; fortunes were made, and fine houses were built. The twentieth century saw their decline as competition from larger operations in central Canada forced the closure of many factories, a series of disasters brought an end to coal mining, and the lumber industry became centralized in mills operated by large corporations. Communities were forced to diversify in order to survive, but traces remain of the industrial heritage that shaped their development.

MILL TOWNS

Nova Scotia's lumber industry was based on the forests that covered the interior, and on the availability of water power to operate sawmills. While most inland communities had one or two sawmills, and often a gristmill too, there were some where the milling of lumber was the chief factor in their development. This exploitation of the forest inevitably impacted the Mi'kmaq, who were deprived of their hunting grounds and gathering places as the settlers' commercial activities encroached on their territories. It became increasingly difficult for Nova Scotia's earlier inhabitants to maintain their former way of life. Hardship and poverty ensued.

Crousetown

The village of Crousetown lies a few kilometres up the Petite Rivière in Lunenburg County, in an area familiar to the Mi'kmaq whose burial ground lay near the estuary. The land along the river was cleared for farming in the 1630s by French settlers from LaHève, as they knew the place, some of whom remained there among their Mi'kmaw friends until at least the end of the century, sharing their traditional way of life. According to one disapproving report, they devoted themselves to hunting and fishing rather than working on their farms, which were left vacant even before the deportation.

In the eighteenth century, a large tract of land on the west side of the Petite Rivière was granted to a syndicate headed by Henry Ferguson, an entrepreneur from Lunenburg, and Antony and Christian Ruhland. These people were speculators; they did not intend to live on their land, which was to be divided into farm lots and sold. The community that grew up at a bend in the river takes its name from a family that bought land there, and whose efforts drove its development. Crousetown's history was largely shaped by the many mills that operated on the river for over a century, most of them by members of the Crouse family.

In 1752, twenty-five-year-old Johann Jacob Kraus and his wife, Maria Clara, left their home in the Palatinate, west of the Rhine, to embark on a journey to Nova Scotia. They were among the Foreign Protestants recruited in the early 1750s to come to Nova Scotia to counterbalance the Roman Catholic Acadians who formed the majority of the population. They arrived in Halifax aboard the *Pearl* and were taken to Lunenburg with their fellow countrymen in 1753. Kraus received a lot in town on which to build a house and a farm lot on First Peninsula, where he and Maria proceeded to raise a family. Their name was anglicized to Crouse. Their second son, Leonard Antony, born in 1758, married Maria Magdalena Gerhardt in 1781. The couple and their family remained in the Lunenburg area until 1797, when they moved to what is now Crousetown.

They were not the first settlers there. Among several earlier land purchasers was Frederick Vogler. His parents, Heinrich and Anna Vogler, were also among the German immigrants who had come to Nova Scotia in the 1750s. Vogler bought a lot from Ferguson in 1777. In 1783, David Dunlop, a Scot, bought a lot on the river from the Ruhlands. Dunlop cleared land for a farm and dug a canal diverting water from the Petite Rivière to create a millrace. Water from this millrace would later power a sawmill and gristmill that sustained much of the area's economy. Dunlop's business failed; he declared bankruptcy in 1797. It was then that Leonard Antony Crouse, seizing the opportunity, sold his land in Lunenburg, and with a partner, Cyrus Martin, bought the Dunlop property which consisted of the farm, barn, mill, and a dwelling. He moved with his wife and children and his young nephew, Gottlieb, to the land on the river that would later be known as Crousetown. His teenaged sons, Leonard Jr., Philip, and Jacob, worked with him in the mill and on the farm, along with their cousin, while his daughters helped their mother in the home. In 1808, Leonard Crouse enlarged his holdings with land purchased from Frederick

Vogler. More settlers came to the area in the nineteenth century, mostly either Foreign Protestant families from Lunenburg or families of Scots-Irish descent who moved upriver from Petite Rivière Bridge.

Over the years, other mills were established and improved as the community expanded. In 1810, Leonard Crouse built a dam across the river and installed a new sawmill and gristmill on the west side. He bought out Cyrus Martin's interest in the old mill lot and sold it with its mill for a nominal sum to Leonard Jr., Gottlieb, and Philip. In 1839, Gottlieb Crouse bought land and built a mill on the east side of the river. A connecting bridge was built below the dam, where today's bridge crosses. At about the same time, Christopher Vogler moved to family property on the river. Other family members joined him and the Voglers ran mills there for many years.

A generation later, the Crouses were still running several of the mills on the river, and the community came to be known as Crousetown Mills. William Leonard Crouse worked in the family business until his death in 1863, when his son, John Will, returned from working at a mill on the Medway to take over the responsibility for his family. John Will became an innovative member of the community. In the early 1860s, he built what was locally known as the "Yanky" sawmill in the middle of the dam. In the early 1870s, he converted the former Dunlop mill, which had changed hands several times, to a gang mill that was capable of sawing multiple boards at a time. He also kept a diary, which depicts much of the daily life of his family and neighbours.

The village gossips must have had a field day in July 1883 when John Will Crouse, then aged thirty-nine, and sixteen-year-old Frances Ramey were married. Unbeknownst to the community, the couple "eloped," as John Will's biographer Robert Mennel puts it, to West Dublin, where the ceremony was performed in St. James's Anglican Church by the Reverend Abraham Jordan in the presence of only two witnesses. John Will returned with his bride and continued to run his business.

By the end of the nineteenth century, Crousetown was enjoying a period of prosperity, with its residents employed in the mills and working their farms. There were now three sawmills clustered beside the bridge. The upper one, with an adjacent lumberyard, was worked by the Voglers and the Hueys. The finished wood from the mills was sent downriver for use in the shipyards at Petite Rivière or loaded there onto vessels to be taken to other markets. On the

Vogler's Oar and Handle Mill, Crousetown's last surviving mill building, still stands by the dam on the Petite Rivière. It is no longer operative.

east side of the river, Gottlieb's son Simeon "Sim" Crouse operated one of the community's two gristmills. The other, on the west side, was run by the Ramey family. The farmers from the surrounding area brought their grain for processing at one or the other of these mills.

In the early twentieth century, Crousetown was still a busy place where mills were worked by the Crouse, Ramey, and Vogler families. Merchant Edwin Eikle ran a lumber business. The Ramey gristmill was bought by William Vogler and his son, who converted it first to a shingle mill and then to an oar and handle mill. The mills were upgraded as technology advanced. Wooden waterwheels gave way to wheels made with a cast iron frame manufactured in Bridgewater and completed locally with wooden parts. In 1904, Beecham and Gideon Crouse installed one of these new wheels in their mill, which had been built before 1840. Another was in use at the Vogler Oar and Handle Mill. In John Will Crouse's later years, his Yanky mill had become an obstruction on the river and had to be dismantled, but he devoted his retirement to building a windmill, perhaps used to pump water to his house or barn. It began to operate in 1910, four years before his death.

The Crousetown mills flourished for much of the twentieth century. There were boom years during the First World War, when there was a high demand for wood, and again in the 1920s, when there was a spurt of house construction in the province. Business dwindled sharply in the 1930s as Nova Scotia was hit hard by the Great Depression, but good times returned when it was over. Beecham and Gideon Crouse's successors, Wilfred and Roy Crouse, ran a planing mill for many years. Grant Crouse returned to Crousetown in 1947, after serving in the Second World War, and he operated a sawmill there for over forty years. His first mill burned down in the 1960s, but he built a new diesel-powered mill that was still turning out lumber in the 1980s.

Time was running out, however, for these small family-operated mills. By the end of the twentieth century, they had all disappeared except for the Vogler Oar and Handle Mill, which still stands at the west end of the Crousetown bridge, though it is no longer operational. The dam that once powered several mills can be seen just above the bridge.

Along the main road through the village, two churches stand a short distance apart. One was originally established in 1887 as a Methodist church, but with Church Union in 1925 it became St. Andrew's United Church. The other is St. Mary's Anglican Church, opened in 1914, whose historic organ built in 1826 is the oldest in use in Nova Scotia. It was brought to St. Mary's and installed in 1963 by the Reverend Dr. Robert Crouse, who for the next forty-seven years organized a series of baroque concerts every summer in the church. Next to the church stands the former one-room Crousetown school, where services were held before the completion of the church.

The chief employer in the community is now the Petite Rivière Vineyards, opened in 2004, with two extensive vineyards planted in 1994 and 1999 respectively on land once farmed by Acadians. Its Provençal-style main building with a terrace and garden is nestled against the hill. Much of the rest of the surrounding farmland has reverted to forest, but a few of the community's gracious old houses remain, including the former Crouse home at the east end of the bridge. Crousetown is now a quiet residential community, but the mill building and dam beside the bridge hark back to its industrial past.

Mill Village

Mill Village lies on the Medway River, on Nova Scotia's South Shore, a few kilometres east of Liverpool. The Medway is one of Nova Scotia's major rivers, running for about 120 kilometres from the interior to Port Medway on the Atlantic coast. It probably took its present name from the one given by the French to the harbour at its mouth, Port Maltois—a port used by Maltese fishing vessels. The name of the port and the river was anglicized to Medway, reminiscent of the English river of that name. The river and harbour were used by the Mi'kmaq for many millennia before Planter settlers established a fishery at the river's mouth in the 1760s.

These settlers' efforts were chiefly devoted to fishing and agriculture, but the vast expanse of forest along the river was a valuable source of timber, and the river itself was a potential source of power for processing wood to feed their budding shipbuilding industry. Early residents Stephen Smith and William Cahoon built a saw- and gristmill on a bend in the river, at a spot known to the Mi'kmaq as Antle'katik, which has been translated as St. Andrews.

The mill was originally funded by a consortium from Liverpool, including diarist and entrepreneur Simeon Perkins. In 1764, a young man named Samuel Mack bought a share in the mill. Mack had recently immigrated to Liverpool from Connecticut, where he had farmed and gained some experience in bridge-building. He came to Port Medway, where he and his second wife, Desire, raised their family: a girl, Elizabeth, and three boys, Samuel, William, and Solomon. (Another son, Stephen, appears not to have survived.) Mack soon bought out the other shareholders and added a second mill to the operations. The business was originally known as Port Medway Mills, and the prosperous milling, lumbering, and farming community that grew up around it became known as Mills Village, later Mill Village. Other sawmills and gristmills were established nearby, serving the lumbermen and farmers of the area.

Samuel Mack's business was doing well when he died in 1783, shortly before his forty-seventh birthday. His wife took over the running of the mills and built a substantial house in Mill Village. Two years after her husband's death, she married Patrick Doran, the business's chief clerk. The house that Desire had built remained in the family for the next century, known for a long time as the Patrick Doran house, and it still stands. It is a registered heritage house, with massive basement walls built with hand-cut stone, four fireplaces and a central chimney, wide floor planks, wooden wall panelling, and original hinges and door locks. An 1825 survey by George Wightman identifies an inn on the main road from Lunenburg to Liverpool as "Mrs. Mack's"; it was run by one of Samuel Mack's daughters-in-law, perhaps Samuel Jr.'s wife, Sophia. In the mid-twentieth century it was operated as the Medway Inn.

The mills and farmland also remained in the family. Samuel Mack's sons worked with their mother, and family members maintained the business until well into the nineteenth century. The population of the village increased, and by 1829, Thomas Haliburton recorded in his two-volume *Historical and Statistical Account of Nova-Scotia*: "Several respectable and wealthy families reside in this place, which contains a number of well-built houses, a spacious methodist [*sic*] chapel, and a schoolhouse. The land in this vicinity is better and more suitable for agriculture than any other part of the township of Liverpool. There are several mills here built on the most approved construction, at which a great quantity of lumber is prepared for exportation. In addition to the other natural resources of this place there is an abundant supply of Alewives of which the inhabitants sometimes take three thousand barrels in one season."

Desire had several children with Patrick. Their daughter Eleanor married Samuel Davison, who continued to operate the farm and sawmill, but they both died young. At the age of twelve, their son, Edward Doran Davison, inherited the property that included farmland, extensive forestland, and the mill. His aunt, Catherine Doran, managed it for him until he was eighteen, when he took control. He was enthusiastic about lumbering and milling, and soon expanded the business, adding one of Nova Scotia's first steam-operated sawmills in 1845. The mill was known as the Old Kettle Mill because of the steam that rose from it. With this and other mills on the river, there was plenty of employment in Mill Village and in the surrounding forest. Oxen hauled loads of logs out of the woods and brought them to the mills, and finished lumber was exported from Port Medway at the river's mouth. Farms were productive, and there was good fishing in the river. The community prospered.

Davison represented Queens County in the legislature from 1854 until 1859 but did not re-offer, and from that time onward devoted himself to his sawmills. He extended his land holdings and maintained the mills over the next twenty years, despite a fire that destroyed much of the timberland in 1849.

The Patrick Doran House, "Mrs. Mack's," was built for Samuel Mack's widow, who married Patrick Doran. It was later run as an inn by the Mack family.

The business flourished for many years under his oversight; however, by 1864, the once–readily available wood supply was diminishing. Davison decided to expand his efforts to the less-developed forests on the LaHave River. With his three sons, he purchased the Glenwood Mill just above Bridgewater, added a second mill further upriver, and developed the most successful lumber business in the province, while retaining an interest in two mills in Mill Village. In 1891, he ordered four new waterwheels from the Yarmouth foundry of the Burrell Johnson Iron Company Works to be installed at one of these, the Village Mill, which was run by Henry Mack, Samuel's great-grandson. Davison became known as the Lumber King of Nova Scotia.

Well-to-do village residents built substantial houses, some of which remain. By the turn of the century, Mill Village had become a well-established community. Lumbering and milling were not the only businesses. A shoe shop stood by the bridge, and there was a telegraph office in a store operated by one of Samuel Mack's descendants. Photographs taken in the early 1900s show two churches and a schoolhouse, stores, and comfortable homes. The road was upgraded and became Trunk 3. The railway line opened from Halifax to Yarmouth, which would become an important factor in the subsequent history of the community.

Changes came later in the twentieth century. The mills were bought by Benjamin Johnstone & Co. and milling continued in the village for some years. But like other communities in Nova Scotia, Mill Village suffered as the demand for lumber fluctuated and became centralized in larger operations. The saw-mills closed, leaving Mill Village without its chief source of employment.

In an unexpected turn of events in the early 1960s, the community changed from a quiet backwater on the South Shore to a major player in the peaceful use of Outer Space, and almost overnight it became a site of international importance. New technology had introduced the use of fixed satellites for communication, and Mill Village was chosen as one of only five places in the world at that time where Earth satellite stations were built. It was selected partly because of its location, isolated from major radio interference, and because of the availability of road and rail transportation to bring in the necessary massive equipment. With its huge dome, satellite dishes, control buildings, and masts, the station sprawled over a large area known as Charleston to the north of the village. It was opened in 1964 and received telephone and television signals from around the world for over twenty years. Pictures of major sporting events and other international items of all kinds were received here and rebroadcast to Canadian television viewers, until further advances in technology made the satellite station redundant. It was shut down in 1985, and over the years the equipment was removed and the buildings wholly or partially demolished. Today, the graffiti-covered ruins are all that is left of what was once a major complex.

Located on the former main road between Lunenburg and Liverpool, Mill Village is now bypassed by Highway 101. To reach it, travellers must take the old road that follows up the river into the village. At the centre, a bridge carries the former Highway 3 across the river, and a combined general store and café beside the bridge serves both residents and passing travellers. Mrs. Mack's Inn has long closed, but Mill Village is still a stopping place for those who enjoy a leisurely exploration of rural Nova Scotia.

Sherbrooke

Many people will be familiar with part of the Nova Scotia Museum complex called Sherbrooke Village, the recreation of a nineteenth-century community in the Eastern Shore's Guysborough County. But the residential area of Sherbrooke is also a living, working community, whose history goes back much further.

St. Marys River, one of Nova Scotia's major rivers, was well known to the Mi'kmaq both as a travel route and as a plentiful source of salmon, the latter of which attracts anglers to its waters to this day. There is said to have been an important Indigenous community near the mouth of the river. The Mi'kmaw name for the area is Napu'saqnuk, meaning "at the place of stringing beads." Beadwork has been an important feature of Mi'kmaw culture since the time of contact with Europeans when they traded furs for manufactured goods. Beads were also used from early days to decorate their clothing and are often incorporated today in jewellery.

French and Basque fishermen undoubtedly knew the river and traded with the Mi'kmaq before Charles Baye, Sieur de la Giraudière, obtained a licence from the Company of New France to establish a fishery and fur-trading post there. The territory to which he laid claim was extensive. In 1658, he set up his headquarters and built a fort at the head of navigation on the river that he named rivière Sainte Marie. A small, fortified trading post grew up, known as Port Sainte Marie, where Sieur de la Giraudière and his men made their living by hunting, fishing, and bartering with their Mi'kmaw neighbours. The fort was enclosed by a picket fence with four bastions. The settlement lasted until 1669, when an English force, led by a French settler with a grudge against Giraudière, raided it, destroyed the fort, seized the occupants, and looted the settlement. Early in the nineteenth century, investigators at the site found the remains of a store, a dwelling, a forge, weapons, tools, and other metal artifacts.

For over one hundred years, the area was once again left to the Mi'kmaq. In the early nineteenth century, settlers began to come to St. Marys River. The Taylor and McKeen families were among the first. James Fisher and his three sons came in 1805, settled at the head of navigation, and built the first sawmill there to process lumber. These early residents were families who had originally moved from Ulster to New Hampshire and thence to Nova Scotia. They were joined by Angus McDonald, a Scot from the Isle of Skye, who had served in the American Revolution. They lived by farming, fishing, and logging. In 1814, David Archibald 3rd, who was also born in New Hampshire, came to the area from Truro, and became the community's leading entrepreneur. He established a farm and a second sawmill and began to develop the lumber business. He also built a gristmill and operated a store. The gristmill was probably established soon after his arrival; it was certainly operating by 1817. It served the population of the surrounding area, and folks came from distant farms to bring their grain for processing.

Archibald exported his lumber by sea and added shipbuilding to his enterprises. Over the next decade, the population increased rapidly. Fishing became less important as residents increasingly turned their attention to the interior, where abundant timber supplies in the forests along the river offered a resource that would drive the future development of the community.

In 1815, the village was known as Sherbrooke, honouring Sir John Coape Sherbrooke, who served as lieutenant-governor of Nova Scotia from 1812 to 1816. By 1818, a post office served the cluster of about twenty houses that made up the community. Sherbrooke was the chief community of St. Marys Township, and in 1819 its residents signed a petition asking that a courthouse be built there. They had to be satisfied with a jail, which was completed the following year. An act of 1840 provided for a Court of General Sessions of the Peace to be held annually at Sherbrooke Court House, as it was originally named. It is not clear when that courthouse was built, but it was replaced by a new building on the same site in 1858, which served until 2000. It stands today, one of the heritage buildings that comprise Sherbrooke Village. The village received a new jail in 1861.

From early days, the residents valued education. Classes were taught in private homes for a few years before David Archibald gave land in 1817 for a combined school and meeting house, which opened the following year. New schools would be built in 1850 and 1867. An Anglican church was consecrated in 1850. The Presbyterians who formed the majority of the population raised funds for a separate church building in 1852; the first service was held three years later. St. James Presbyterian Church still stands in the restored Sherbrooke Village.

Lumbering and shipbuilding were at the centre of the community's economy in the 1820s. Logs were floated downriver in rafts to the village's sawmills, and sawn lumber from mills higher upriver came down in the same way. Booms on the river at Sherbrooke controlled the passage of logs and caught anything that broke loose. There had been shipyards on the river since Elisha Pride and Robert Dickson built a schooner in 1813. Vessels built there were used for fishing and for shipping lumber to market. A large amount of lumber was exported to England, and merchants brought in goods to supply the population. One of David Archibald's sons, William Thompson Archibald, in partnership with Henry Cumminger, built a new sawmill in the village in 1829. It was powered by a millrace bringing water from a lake above the village. The MacDonald brothers bought the mill in about 1850, and it changed hands again forty years later but burned down. It had been abandoned by the end of the century.

In the 1830s, business in the community had slowed. When Joseph Howe paid a visit in 1831, he found "a rough and unsightly cluster of houses" where he had difficulty in locating a blacksmith to re-shoe his horse. Sherbrooke's economy seemed to be in a slump. "At one time," Howe wrote in his collected *Western and Eastern Rambles*, "it was the scene of an active and profitable trade in lumber and new vessels, ten, of from fifty to one hundred tons, having been built there in a few years. In 1824, 25 and 26, fourteen cargoes of timber, amounting in the whole to 4155 tons, 63,000 feet of plank, besides, lath wood, spars, etc., and in 1827, 400,000 feet of sawed lumber, and 100 head of horned cattle were sent from this place to Halifax." But now shipbuilding was in a decline, as Howe noted: "There are now two or three small vessels in the stocks and the whole business of the place appears to be their completion, and the rafting, sawing of timber." But Howe remarked on the new sawmill with approval: "There is an excellent Saw Mill at the lower extremity of the village, which is supplied with water through a sort of canal, cut for a distance of a quarter of a mile, to the margin of a lake."

Sherbrooke merchants continued to export lumber and import consumer goods by sea. But to develop as a trading centre, adequate communication by

The reconstructed MacDonald Mill in Sherbrooke Village is a fine example of a working water-powered sawmill.

land was also necessary. For many years, the community had been relatively isolated; a road of sorts had existed along St. Marys River since the early days of settlement, but there was no road along the Eastern Shore. It was not until 1850 that demand was answered with a road known as the Great Eastern constructed between Halifax and Guysborough, including a branch following the old route down the river to Sherbrooke.

This improvement to communications allowed the community to develop rapidly in the 1860s. By 1861, the population had expanded considerably, and Sherbrooke was established as the administrative centre of the district. That same year, gold was discovered on the west side of the river, attracting hopeful prospectors to the area known as Goldenville, and bringing a wave of business to Sherbrooke's hotels and boarding houses. There were three sawmills, a tannery, carriage shops, merchants and shopkeepers, blacksmiths, carpenters, shipwrights, and a variety of tradesmen. A gold commissioner was one of several officials established in the village by the mid-1860s, including a controller of customs, a postmaster, and a surveyor of shipping. The ferry across St. Marys River was kept busy, and stagecoach services linked Sherbrooke with Halifax, Antigonish, and Mulgrave. In 1870, a bridge across the river replaced the ferry service.

The 1860s were the time of Sherbrooke's greatest prosperity. After that, the gold rush was over. Production slowed as the seams at Goldenville became exhausted, and the population dropped again. By the end of the century, the era of wooden ships was also ending. Nonetheless, a new sawmill was built, and the lumber export industry remained a major part of the economy into the twentieth century.

Sherbrooke's population continued to decline. By the 1950s, there were only about three hundred residents. In a major development during the following decade, a contingent of residents started plans to create a restored Sherbrooke Village as a museum site alongside the existing community. Work began in 1970: buildings were moved, reconstructed, or restored to recreate village life as it was in its prosperous days. The restoration today includes historic homes, businesses that operated in the nineteenth century, and trades and crafts once practised. The MacDonald sawmill was reconstructed and made operational. Authentic period artifacts were acquired, including a hand-operated printing press. Local interpreters in costume demonstrate the daily lives and skills of early residents. The courthouse, one of the village's showpieces, remained in use until 2000 and is now home to a summer concert series.

Sherbrooke Village has become a major tourist attraction, hosting visitors from all over the world, bolstering the economy of this historic community. Some people still live in the restored village, but the residential area of Sherbrooke is a modern community, involved with forestry, lumbering, and carpentry. Its amenities include a hospital, regional school, church, bank, post office, stores, tourist accommodation, and restaurants. Today's Sherbrooke coexists comfortably with its nineteenth-century counterpart.

MINING AND MANUFACTURING

The discovery of coal and iron ore brought profound transformations to some former rural inland communities. Coal not only heated people's homes but also provided fuel for furnaces that smelted iron and powered the steam engines that ran factory machinery. Communities expanded rapidly as miners, iron-workers, and other skilled tradesmen were brought in to live and work in com-pany towns. They were forced to buy necessities with credit at the company stores, which profited from their purchases, and they often found themselves with little left from their wage packets by the time they had paid their bills. Mining was hard, dangerous work, and there were many accidents under-ground, as well as some major disasters. Nevertheless, men came in search of work. Mining and manufacturing became the economic drivers of certain com-munities toward the end of the nineteenth century. These industries began to decline, however, in the twentieth century, when some could no longer compete with larger operations in central Canada and the United States. Coal mines proved too dangerous to be maintained, and demand for fossil fuels dropped off. Nova Scotia's industrial past has given way to a more diverse economy.

The Stellarton/New Glasgow Industrial Area

The East River of Pictou is the longest of three that run into Pictou Harbour, and it has for thousands of years provided a route from the interior of Nova Scotia to the sea. The Mi'kmaq, who were among the earliest inhabitants, used it to travel between inland hunting grounds and the seafood-rich harbour.

The earliest settlers on the East River were Scots who came to Pictou on the *Hector* in 1773, but the population gradually spread southward. After the American Revolution, lots on what was known as the Soldiers Grant, some distance up the East River, were given to the Mackay brothers—Donald, Roderick, and William—who had come on the *Hector*. They all played import-ant roles in the growth of the community: Donald, known as Donald the builder, was later ordained an elder, or deacon, of the Presbyterian Church; Roderick was a blacksmith by trade; and the third brother, known as "Squire" William Mackay, became a Justice of the Peace. They were joined by two other brothers: Alexander, the oldest, and Hugh. By 1785, the Mackays owned much of the land on both sides of the river. Their neighbours were mostly fellow Highlanders who had fought in the war; their first, and for most their only, language was Gaelic. When Surveyor General Charles Morris II surveyed the area that same year, he noted on his "Plan of Surveys made & Lands Granted… at Merigumish [sic] & Pictou" that "by proper Attention & industry this district will become a Valuable Settlement." He could not have foreseen just how valuable it would become.

In 1786, a newcomer arrived in the area. A young Presbyterian clergyman, the Reverend James MacGregor, who spoke both English and Gaelic, was sent as a missionary from Scotland to serve his fellow countrymen at Pictou. MacGregor had assumed that he would be coming to an established town but found only log cabins strung out on Pictou's three rivers. He conducted his first service near the harbour, but his first pastoral visit was to the Highlanders of the East River.

He established two churches, one of them at the Mackay settlement on the East River, and the other at Loch Broom on the West River. He travelled between them to conduct services, an arrangement that lasted for some years, until in 1795 a new minister, the Reverend Duncan Ross, arrived in the area and was appointed to the church at Loch Broom, while MacGregor made his home on the west bank of the East River. His house stood beside a bridge that linked the road from Musquodoboit, known as the Governor's Road, to the road toward Pictou. Like other ministers of his time, he operated a small farm to help feed his family. He was married twice and raised nine children.

MacGregor was a practical man, so when he discovered small outcrops of coal on his property, he obtained a licence to mine them. For over twenty years, he used coal to heat his house. His neighbour, William Mackay, had also obtained a licence, but serious mining in the area began only in 1825, when the rights for mineral development in Nova Scotia were accorded to the General Mining Association. When the company purchased MacGregor's land west of the river, he built a new home on the east side, near the church.

The purchase by the General Mining Association marked the beginning of a period of intense industrial development in the area. The company's manager, Richard Smith, brought experienced miners from England and built a fine house for himself, known as Mount Rundell, where he entertained many distinguished guests. A company town was established for the workers, with a school, a chapel, medical facilities, and the inevitable company store, which took back most of the workers' wages. Joseph Howe, visiting in 1830, observed in *Western and Eastern Rambles* that he found "a range of brick and a number of wooden tenements where the Miners and their families reside."

The community was originally known as Albion Mines and would later become Stellarton. Mining equipment, including a steam-operated pump and a steam locomotive known as Samson, was brought in. Coal production began in 1827. Samson hauled coal cars on the Albion Railway from the mines to the loading docks at the head of navigation. Howe noted the rail line to the New Glasgow wharf and the engine house with steam-operated machinery that hauled coal up from the mine. He even went down into the mine to inspect it personally. By 1838, steam engines were powering many of the mine's operations, including the steamboats that carried coal from New Glasgow to be loaded onto ships at Pictou. The industry expanded as new coal seams were discovered, including one on James MacGregor's former property, known as the MacGregor Seam, and the Foord Seam, said to be the thickest in the world. Neighbouring Westville developed as a second coal-mining town after coal was found there in 1864. The Nova Scotia Railway line was extended in 1867 and began to carry coal directly from the mines to the wharf at Pictou Landing for export by sea.

The General Mining Company's monopoly was revoked in 1858, but other investors operated the mines, and coal remained the basis of the economy until the late twentieth century. Although the mines provided work, miners were poorly paid and were forced to live on credit from the company stores. Children were employed in mines from an early age, and often continued there for all of their working lives. Poor working conditions and inadequate wages sometimes resulted in strikes. Inevitably, miners returned to work with little or no improvement.

Mining is a dangerous business. This area saw more than its share of disasters over the years. Rockfalls killed and injured miners, and fires and explosions frequently occurred in Stellarton's mines, caused by methane leaking from the coal seams, and often compounded by inadequate safety precautions. In 1873, the Westville Mine saw the loss of sixty-six lives. In 1918, an explosion in Stellarton's Allan Mine resulted in the death of eighty-eight miners.

The Foord Pit in Albion Mines. The Foord coal seam, 13.5 metres thick, was said to be the thickest in the world.

The final blow came in 1992, when a major explosion in the Westray Mine in nearby Plymouth killed twenty-six men. After this disaster, which was caused partly by neglect of proper safety measures, the dangerous nature of the work was recognized as unacceptable. The accident triggered some reforms in the mining industry, but at the same time, the demand for coal as a source of power dropped off. Toward the end of the century, the coal mines began to close.

Downriver from Albion Mines, Deacon Thomas Fraser had settled in 1784 on the west side of the river, at the head of navigation. Here, a community of Scots grew up at what would become known as New Glasgow. Like other settlers, they cleared land, built log cabins, and started farms. In 1809, James William Carmichael and George Amos set up a trading post, which marked the beginning of commercial activities in the community as goods were brought upriver in small vessels, unloaded at New Glasgow's wharves, and sold to residents of the surrounding region.

This community, once home to Highland settlers in their log cabins, became both the transfer point for the region's coal exports and a manufacturing centre. In 1840, George MacKenzie's shipbuilding company was established. New Glasgow's major industry was spurred by the discovery of iron ore on nearby McLennan Brook. Other iron ore deposits were subsequently found, along with sources of hematite, used in the smelting process. The New Glasgow Iron Foundry and the I. Matheson & Company's Acadia Iron Foundry began operating in the 1860s. The Hope Iron Works was established in 1872. Other industries followed, and New Glasgow quickly grew up as the commercial centre of an important industrial area. By the end of the century, the Matheson plant was making steam-powered tugboats, and steel was being produced at what would become Trenton. Steam-operated sawmill machinery and tram locomotives for handling lumber were manufactured by Alex McPherson in New Glasgow.

The surrounding forests remained a source of timber, and in the late nineteenth century there were several woodworking factories producing doors, window sashes, and other building supplies. In 1871, the machinery in Alexander Robertson's cabinetmaking shop was still powered by two horses who walked for hours round a vertical shaft that turned the gears. Soon steam became the source of power for New Glasgow's industries. J. W. Carmichael's New Glasgow shipyard was using a steam-powered mill in the 1880s. In 1897, Alex McPherson began to manufacture stationary and portable steam-powered sawmills. Several of these operated in Stellarton and New Glasgow in the late nineteenth century.

In 1881, William Godkin Beach came to Nova Scotia to look for a place to establish a factory that would produce glass tableware, the first to do so in Canada. The availability of coal in the New Glasgow area resulted in him establishing the Nova Scotia Glass Company in Trenton. Beach constructed his factory, imported machinery and a gas furnace that operated with cheap second grade coal, and recruited experienced glass workers. He began by making blown glass lamp chimneys and globes for lanterns, but soon began to produce the pressed glass tableware for which his company became known. In 1890, two more glass factories were opened: the Lamont Glass Company specialized in coloured glass and lamp chimneys, while the Humphreys Glass Works made jars and bottles. The Nova Scotia and Lamont Glass Companies were bought by a Montreal company and were closed by the turn of the century, but the Humphreys firm continued to operate in Trenton until 1917.

In the present century, the mining and manufacturing that were once at the heart of the area's prosperity have come to an end. In Stellarton's Museum of Industry, visitors can follow the development and decline of one of Nova Scotia's major industrial areas.

Springhill

Until 1958, not many Canadians beyond Nova Scotia had ever heard of a town in the Cobequid Mountains of Cumberland County called Springhill, and probably not many Nova Scotians could have placed it accurately on a map. It received its name because it lies on a hill where water once trickled out of the ground in a series of springs. It became known not for its springs but for its coal mining, which ended in 1958 with a disastrous explosion in the No. 2 Colliery that drew national and international media coverage.

The first settlers who came to Springhill in 1770 were not looking for coal, although "coal cliffs" had been identified in the Joggins area of Cumberland County many years before. The pioneers cleared land for farming and were joined in the 1780s by Loyalist families in the aftermath of the American Revolution. They soon realized as they worked their fields that their land held another resource: coal. They dug surface coal as fuel for their fires. A small mine opened in 1834, but large-scale commercial development was delayed. For many years Springhill remained a community of farmers and loggers.

Springhill's first school was established in 1817 by William Willeford, a mathematician and astronomer who later became a professor in Memphis, Tennessee. The school was known simply as Willeford's School. There seems to have been considerable interest in education, as several other privately operated schools sprang up later in the nineteenth century to meet the increase in population. The first churches were built in the second half of the century: a Methodist church was opened in 1863, a Baptist church in 1883, and All Saints Anglican in 1892.

After the original mine opened on the coalfield, further development occurred only gradually. The General Mining Association, which had acquired rights to exploit minerals in all of Nova Scotia in 1825, lost most of these rights in 1858 when, as a result of public pressure, a bill was passed in the Nova Scotia Legislature rescinding them. The company retained assets on the Springhill coalfield, but because this inland area was without a major river to facilitate exporting the coal, it was in no hurry to develop the resource.

Without the means of shipping by water, the only way coal could be carried to market was by an overland route. Interest in opening mines in the area first arose in the late 1860s, when the Intercolonial Railway was under construction, passing a short distance to the north of Springhill. Railcars would provide the means to exploit coal resources, and in the 1870s the Springhill and Parrsboro Coal and Railway Company made plans to mine coal and export it by building a rail line. The line would run southward through the mountains and down the valley of Farrells River to the port of Parrsboro. From there, coal could be shipped to destinations in Nova Scotia and the United States. A line to the north would connect with the Intercolonial Railway, and commercial mining in the Springhill coalfield could begin.

To encourage development of the coalfield, the government provided a subsidy for the railway in 1874, and construction began the following year. Once an export route had been established, the company obtained mineral rights to an area of Crown land adjacent to the General Mining Association's property. Workers were brought in, and the mining community of Springhill was born. The railway opened in 1877, and shipments of coal to Parrsboro began, while coal was also carried by the Intercolonial line from Springhill Junction.

The General Mining Association's rights to the adjoining area were revoked in 1879, further reducing their interests in the province, and transferred to the Springhill and Parrsboro Company, which expanded its operations accordingly. By 1884, the company had run into financial difficulties, and its assets were purchased by the Cumberland Railway and Coal Company. Development of the Springhill coalfield was further expanded with the opening of two new mines, known as No. 1 and No. 2.

In those days, mining was carried out by hand with picks, requiring a large labour force including young children, and the community grew rapidly in the way of all mining towns. To accommodate the miners, company houses were built, along with a company store. Churches, schools, and other services were established, and the town of Springhill Mines was incorporated in 1889. Given the dangerous nature of coal extraction, it was only two years later that the first mining disaster took place. No. 1 and No. 2 mines at Springhill were joined by a connecting tunnel, and accumulated coal dust in the two collieries caught fire, causing an explosion. Despite rescue operations, 125 miners, some of them children, were killed, and many more were injured.

Production resumed after this disaster. By the end of the nineteenth century, the mines were worked on an even larger scale and the population of Springhill Mines increased accordingly. In 1910, the Cumberland Railway and Coal Company was absorbed as a subsidiary by the Dominion Coal Company Limited, which in its turn was merged into the British Empire Steel Corporation in 1920. Ten years later, the latter became part of the Dominion Steel and Coal Corporation. Throughout the course of all these changes new mines were opened, and large-scale coal production continued until the 1950s, when demand began to decline as oil and electricity became the major sources of domestic heating, and diesel locomotives replaced coal-burning steam engines.

Springhill's second major mining disaster took place in 1956. Coal dust was regularly hauled out from working areas of the mine by trains running on tracks along the shafts. On November 1, one of these trains was carrying dust from No. 4 Colliery when a blast of air from the ventilation system blew the dust around, spreading it through the mine. Some of the train's cars broke loose, ran back down the shaft, derailed, and hit a power line. The resulting sparks ignited the dispersed coal dust and caused a fire and an explosion 1,700 metres below the surface. Over one hundred miners were trapped in the shaft by fallen timbers and debris.

While anxious families waited at the pithead, miners known as drae-germen wearing protective equipment worked alongside barefaced miners with just their normal implements. They made their way to the trapped men by way of a lower level of the mine and were able to bring eighty-eight of them safely to the surface. Sadly, another thirty-nine perished. The fire continued to burn for some time, and it was not until the following January that the bodies of the victims were recovered.

As the lyrics of "The Ballad of Springhill," by Peggy Seeger and Ewan MacColl, suggest, there was often a feeling of unease in the mining area of Springhill. The town was known for its "bumps" caused by earth movements around the mined areas. By 1958, the years of mining had created a vast network

The draegermen entering the Springhill mine in 1956 after the explosion that trapped more than one hundred men were miners specially equipped for rescue work.

of underground tunnels where the ground sometimes shifted a little, causing a bump. These events were not uncommon, so when one occurred on October 23 in No. 2 Colliery, the men working there were not especially worried. But just over an hour later, a major bump with shock waves on par with an earthquake shook the town, and residents realized immediately that something serious had occurred. Families and rescue teams rushed to the scene, where they found some men making their way out of the mine. Catastrophe had indeed struck: some miners had been crushed as the shafts collapsed, while others were trapped by rockfalls and debris.

Teams of rescuers came as before from mines in other areas to join the searchers. The town's residents pitched in to support them, offering food and lodging. After five and a half days, contact was made with the first group of twelve survivors, who were living in darkness without food or water and had almost given up hope of rescue. They were brought to the surface the following day. After another two days, a second group was found; they would be the last. In all, seventy-five men lost their lives. This final disaster led to the closure of the Cumberland mine.

The event attracted unprecedented publicity. The rescue efforts were televised by CBC and reported by Canadian and international news media. Prince Philip, who was in Canada at the time, visited the site with then-premier of Nova Scotia Robert Stanfield. The town of Springhill received the Carnegie

Medal for heroism. Books have been written based on the event, and folksingers Seeger and MacColl composed and sang "The Ballad of Springhill." It has since been performed many times, by many singers.

Another singer has kept the community's name before the public. Anne Murray was born in Springhill in 1945, became a popular performer in the 1960s with CBC's *Singalong Jubilee*, and went on to a successful singing career, performing extensively and selling millions of records. She received the Order of Canada in 1984. The Anne Murray Centre in Springhill opened in 1989, attracting fans of her music and boosting the town's economy.

Change has come to Springhill since the closure of the Cumberland mine. In 1967, as part of the policy of diversifying the town's economy, a medium security penitentiary, known as the Springhill Institution, was opened on a plateau overlooking the town. It is the largest fenced correctional facility in Canada.

The mines have left an interesting legacy in Springhill. Companies have made use of geothermal energy provided by warm water from the flooded mine shafts since the 1980s. In the last few years, plans have been developed for a new "green" geothermal industrial park to attract businesses to the area. People come to the Springhill Coal Mining National Historic Site and the Springhill Miners' Museum, where they can learn more about the history of the mines, the work of miners, and the tragedies that took the lives of so many in this community.

Londonderry

The area of the Cobequid Mountains where Londonderry Township was established in the early 1860s was home to some of Nova Scotia's earliest Indigenous people. It is not far from the Debert Paleo-Indian Site, where evidence has been found of settlement from between 10,500 and 11,000 years ago, making it the oldest archaeological site in the province. The artifacts found there include stone weapons and tools, made by distant ancestors of today's Mi'kmaq. The region's rivers served as highways for Indigenous travellers, and Londonderry stands on the upper part of the Great Village River where Mi'kmaw canoes had passed for many thousands of years before white men arrived.

With a name like Londonderry, it is not surprising to learn that the first European settlers in this part of Nova Scotia were of Irish descent. Their ancestors had moved from Scotland to Ulster, and from there they had immigrated to New Hampshire, where they established the community of Londonderry. In 1761, when New Englanders were responding to Governor Lawrence's invitation to take up land in Nova Scotia, Alexander McNutt brought a group of these Scots-Irish settlers from New Hampshire to populate a new township between Cobequid Bay and the Cobequid Mountains. They were joined a few years later by another Scots-Irish group, who had sailed to Nova Scotia in 1761 on board the *Hopewell*, which happened to be out of Londonderry, Ireland. The township was clearly destined to be called Londonderry.

While some of the pioneers who arrived at the Port of Londonderry (now Great Village) took up grants along the shore where Acadians had previously developed farms, others moved inland. They were granted lots along the river valley and made their living by farming and logging. By 1784, the Denneys, Dills, McLeans, McLellans, Reaghs, Skinners, and others owned lots along the road through the valley. Lumber was processed at a mill at Great Village, at the mouth of the river of the same name.

This rural way of life continued well into the nineteenth century, with newcomers joining the township's farming community, while some of the earlier settlers scattered or moved away. Change began in 1844, when veins of iron ore were discovered in the upper part of the Great Village River valley. Two years later, with the help of English investors, the Acadia Charcoal Iron Company was incorporated. The manager, a Welshman named Thomas Butler, oversaw the installation of a water-powered crusher at the point where the Rockland Brook and the Great Village River came together, and forges, furnaces, and other smelting equipment were set up to process the ore. Exploration of the exposed seams continued, and men were brought in to mine the ore at what became known as Acadia Mines.

These immigrant workers formed the nucleus of what soon became a busy community. The iron manufacturing plant grew, and by 1850 it was in production with a new manager, John Blanchard. As the business expanded, a typical company town grew up beside the ironworks. It comprised a fine house on the hill for the general manager, comfortable homes for managerial staff, and several rows of cheaply built cottages for the workers.

The iron that came from the smelters was of high quality and found a ready market in Britain. It had to be carried by horse or ox cart down the valley to the Port of Londonderry, where it was loaded onto vessels for shipping to the English cutlery manufacturers at Sheffield. There was also a demand from British gun makers for pig iron, but after its initial success, the Londonderry iron plant had a checkered history. The management changed several times in the first few years, and there were financial worries. By 1860, the Acadia Charcoal and Iron Company had been restructured and new equipment was installed, making it more efficient.

After Confederation, with the promise of a railway line to central Canada, the company was again restructured as the Intercolonial Iron and Steel Company. In 1869, the plant began producing steel wheels for the Intercolonial Railway's cars. In 1872, the opening of a spur line linking Acadia Mines with the railway's main line provided a long-awaited export route. The following year, the British-based Steel Company of Canada took over operations. Its chairman, William Siemens, brought expansion and innovations to the business, building a new steel plant, and incorporating some experimental projects. He introduced the more efficient Bessemer process for making steel, which was used in Acadia Mines for the first time in Canada. The community seemed destined for prosperity, but Siemens's experiments were not always successful.

Mining operations also expanded as new ore seams were opened. Three mines (the Old Mountain Mine, and the East and West Mines) were worked by miners brought in from elsewhere in Nova Scotia, and from Britain, the United States, and beyond. In order to keep the plant working at full capacity, an additional 120 miners were brought from the Cornish tin mines. The ore was transported in railcars along a railway built from the East and West Mines to the steel plant.

One of Siemens's less successful experiments was an attempt to produce steel directly from iron ore without the usual preliminary smelting operations. It may have seemed like a good idea at the time, but it proved to be expensive and impracticable. The company had to be restructured once again, with further changes: new equipment was installed, including a rolling mill and blast furnace. In 1876, coke replaced charcoal for the furnace and over sixty brick-built "beehive" coke ovens were installed to process coal brought from the Albion Mines at Stellarton. But trouble came when workers' wages were reduced as part of the restructuring, and a violent strike ensued, resulting in the death of one worker. Troops had to be sent in from Halifax to quell the unrest.

Production resumed after this disruption, and the 1870s and '80s were the busiest times for the Acadia Mines community, with employment at its highest level. The population increased to around five thousand, consisting of miners, steelworkers, management staff, and people serving community needs. The company operated a hotel, a barbershop, and recreation facilities, as well as the usual company store. The general manager lived in the grand house over-looking the works and the town; his staff and well-to-do citizens had comfort-able homes, while the workers lived in the rows of company houses clustered together near the works site. There were three churches: Roman Catholic, Baptist, and Methodist. The community was at the height of its prosperity.

In 1902, the town of Acadia Mines was officially renamed Londonderry, but by this time the boom was over. The iron ore seams had proved to be less productive than expected, and Ontario was mining extensive iron ore deposits with which Londonderry could not compete. The mines closed in 1898 but were shortly reopened with yet another restructuring as the Londonderry Iron and Mining Company. In 1900, even before production began, a major fire destroyed the plant's foundry, rolling mills, and pipe shop. Reconstruction took place once again, but hopes for a permanent revival of the community's steel industry in the new century were doomed to disappointment. World prices were low, and even after further restructuring, it became difficult to continue with any profits by manufacturing steel. From that time on, production was limited, and workers were laid off. The final blow came in 1920, when another serious fire destroyed many of the town's buildings. Londonderry never recov-ered from this second disaster. Iron-ore mining continued for a few more years but ended in 1924 as production became unprofitable. The ironworks were sold for scrap and the buildings were demolished.

Inevitably, most of the people who had been employed in the ironworks and the mines moved away to seek employment elsewhere. The economy of Londonderry was based solely on the mining and processing of iron ore. Once this was over, there was no alternative source of employment in this isolated community. The town that was once home to five thousand people has dimin-ished to around two hundred, most of whom now work in nearby Debert. All

The blast furnace at Londonderry's iron plant processed the ore into pig iron in the early twentieth century.

that is left of the former iron-mining and steel-making industries are scattered outcrops of ore, the remains of some beehive furnaces, and a slag heap. In a small memorial park, there is a monument to workers who lost their lives in the mines or ironworks, and a few pieces of equipment from the former industrial community are displayed. The community's industrial past has vanished, leaving a ghost town. Despite its checkered history, Londonderry can proudly claim that some of the first steel manufactured in Canada was produced here.

Amherst

The town of Amherst lies southeast of the Missaguash River, which today marks the border between Nova Scotia and New Brunswick. In the 1750s, during the Seven Years War, the river separated the French and the British armies and was the scene of fighting between the two forces. Just north of today's town of Amherst, the Acadian village of Beaubassin was founded by

Jacques Bourgeois and a group of families from Port Royal in about 1670. By 1755, its inhabitants had already been driven from their homes, not by English soldiers but by Indigenous followers of Abbé Le Loutre.

Le Loutre was a French priest who had come to Nova Scotia to establish a mission for the Indigenous inhabitants, but he did not confine himself to spiritual matters. Taking a political stance, he persuaded his Mi'kmaw followers to join Acadian activists in conducting guerilla warfare against the British. The British Fort Lawrence at Beaubassin faced Fort Beauséjour on the French side of the Missaguash River. When a British attack seemed imminent in 1755, Le Loutre's followers drove the residents of Beaubassin across into French territory and burned their homes and farms to the ground to prevent their return, and to prevent any use by the British. The French were defeated in the battle that ensued, and most of the Acadians who had lived in Nova Scotia for generations were deported.

In the 1760s, when settlers were brought to Nova Scotia to replace the Acadians, a town began to develop just south of Beaubassin. It was the site of a former Mi'kmaw encampment, on a rise overlooking the extensive dyke lands drained by the Acadians. The town, like many other colonial settlements, was named for an English statesman, in this case Lord Jeffery Amherst, who has since become notorious for his letters advocating the spreading of smallpox among the Indigenous peoples of North America. The town's name is now a subject of controversy.

The early population consisted of New England settlers and a contingent of British immigrants from Yorkshire, some Irish, and a few Acadians who had been allowed to return to Nova Scotia in 1764. They first established themselves west of the present town and built a church, shops, a tavern, and a black-smith shop; the amenities included a whipping post. The residents were joined after the American Revolution by both Black and white Loyalists. Some of the Black settlers came as slaves of white families, while others had earned their freedom by fighting on the British side. When a gristmill and a tannery were built farther to the east, the centre of population moved to what was known as Morses Corner, or Amherst Corner, where houses were built that formed the nucleus of the present town. The surrounding area was farmland.

In 1818, the Amherst area bore the brunt of a fierce storm. Lord Dalhousie, the lieutenant-governor, happened to be on his way there at the time. He recorded the event in his journal:

As we approached [Amherst], the day extremely sultry, the sky o'ercast &
gathered a very wild appearance, & about 4 o'clock one of the most awful
Thunder storms I ever saw set in with violent gusts of wind, vivid flashes
of lightning & instant crash. One particularly loud seemed to burst close
around us,...another followed almost instant & in our view darting like a
spiral rod of fire struck a pine tree on the side of the road & shivered it to
pieces about 200 yards from where we stood.
    [The following day his party surveyed the damage:]
    Under a grove of spruce, fir, perhaps 20 trees, some sheep had taken
shelter & with them a cow and a pig. The electric fluid had struck in the
midst of the trees, apparently conducted down two of them, & then diverg-
ing in every direction had killed on the spot every one of the animals—32
sheep, 1 cow, 1 pig...on all of the sheep there was a line singed as if by a hot
iron from the hind leg into the head.

No doubt this storm was remembered in Amherst for many years.

The community remained relatively isolated until 1842, when a two-horse stagecoach began to run from Truro twice weekly. Before that time, mail had been delivered by a horse and wagon. By 1852, the service had increased to three times a week, and in 1860 a coach met the train at the Truro station and picked up passengers for Amherst every day except Sunday. The journey across the Cobequid Mountains took fifteen hours. It was not until 1872 that the Intercolonial Railway line brought train service directly to Amherst, where a wooden station was built.

The railway provided a much-needed link to markets, and Amherst quickly developed into a busy industrial town during the last quarter of the nineteenth century. One of the chief drivers of the economy for many years was the Rhodes Curry Company. In 1877, Nelson Admiral Rhodes established a woodworking company in his native Amherst in partnership with his brother-in-law Nathaniel Curry, and Barry Dodge. They originally specialized in manufacturing wooden sashes and doors but soon expanded into general construction, buying up mills and brick plants to manufacture their materials. The company built both private houses and public buildings in many parts of the Maritime provinces. Dodge left the business after a few years, and in the 1880s the remaining partners added the repair of railcars to their activities. The Rhodes Curry Company began manufacturing freight cars and passenger coaches in 1891 and continued to do so for many years, becoming the major employer in Amherst. After Nelson Rhodes's death in 1909, the company amalgamated with the Dominion Car and Foundry and the Canadian Car and Foundry companies. Business flourished in the early twentieth century. The First World War brought a flurry of activity, but manufacturing slowed after the war. It picked up again in the Second World War, when the factory turned out airplanes. Work dropped off again when peace returned. The business closed in the 1950s.

Another major contributor to Amherst's growth as an industrial town was the Robb Engineering Works, founded in 1848 as a general metalworking company producing mining and lumbering machinery. Their foundry made stoves and other cast-iron products. The company went on to produce boilers, electric engines, and generators, and to design and manufacture locomotive engines. Robb Engineering in its turn became part of larger businesses, as it was bought by the Dominion Bridge Company, which in turn merged into the Canadian Car and Foundry Company.

Amherst was home to a wide variety of other industries in the late nineteenth and early twentieth centuries. The Christie Baggage company produced a variety of trunks and suitcases from 1863 until 1968, and provided the town with a swimming pool and bathhouse with steam-heated water. The Amherst Boot and Shoe Company was incorporated in 1867 and later amalgamated with a tannery and a second shoe company to become the Amherst Boot, Shoe and Tanning Company. Business flourished in the early twentieth century, but the general slump in the economy in the 1920s brought serious losses, and the plant closed in 1927. The Hewson Woollen Mills, established in 1902, manufactured high-quality woollen goods for about ten years before being taken over by the Stanfield company of Truro to turn out cloth, blankets, and yarn.

Other businesses that brought prosperity to Amherst in the past were a piano factory, a brickworks, a carriage factory and livery stables, blacksmith's shops and farriers, quarries, and a short-lived motorworks where the MacKay car was manufactured for a year. There were woodworks, graniteworks, a mineral water plant, and an electricity company. Busy Amherst had hotels, restaurants, and saloons, and a wide variety of retail shops. It became the administrative centre for Cumberland County. Its courthouse was built in 1889. Services to the population included a town hall, a post office, schools, and churches.

Town of Amherst, 1876, *by A. J. Hill. Four of the six churches reported to be operating at this time can be seen here.*

During the nineteenth and early twentieth centuries, the prosperous citizens of Amherst built fine homes along Victoria Street, some of which still stand. Among them is "Victoria," built in 1907 for Edgar Hewson, the owner of the woollen mill. Amherst was home to many distinguished residents, including four Fathers of Confederation—an unusually high number for any one town. They included Sir Charles Tupper, a doctor-turned-politician who served as premier of Nova Scotia from 1864 to 1867 and brought the province into Confederation. He was elected to the Canadian Parliament where he served in numerous offices; he became Canada's prime minister for a short time, from 1895 to 1896. Robert Barry Dickey was a lawyer and businessman who became a judge and Queen's Counsel. He was elected to Nova Scotia's Legislative Council and was selected by Tupper to attend the Quebec and Charlottetown Conferences that preceded Confederation—to which he was initially opposed. He was appointed to the Senate in 1867. Jonathan McCully was an Amherst lawyer who moved to Halifax where he became a journalist and newspaper owner, writing in support of Confederation. He was appointed to the Legislative Council and held several public offices, including that of Railway Commissioner at the time when the Nova Scotia Railway was being built. After attending the Charlottetown Conference, he, too, was appointed to the Senate. Although Edward Barron Chandler, Amherst's fourth Father of Confederation, was born in the town, he moved to New Brunswick as a young man to study law. He was a member of the legislature and the Legislative Council and represented New Brunswick at the Quebec and Charlottetown Conferences. He refused a Senate appointment, but later became the province's lieutenant-governor.

Just as industries of other Maritime towns declined in the twentieth century, so too did Amherst's, as manufacturing became concentrated in larger areas in central Canada. Today, the town is home to a variety of new businesses, as well as a service centre for the surrounding agricultural area. Its courthouse is the centre of justice in Cumberland County. Many other historic buildings are still standing, some of them now repurposed. The hospitality industry is active, welcoming tourists from all parts of Canada who come across the nearby border with New Brunswick.

Oxford

Oxford lies on River Philip, called by the Mi'kmaq Kesooskiboogwek ("flowing through the hemlock"), which served as a major transportation route for both Indigenous travellers and the early European settlers. The town, like its counterpart in England, derives its name from the shallow river crossing used by oxen in early days. And like its namesake, it is located on a low-lying floodplain, but the two places have little else in common.

Nova Scotia's Oxford dates back to the early 1790s, when settler Richard Thompson arrived from what is now New Brunswick with his wife, Dorothy; their three teenaged sons, Ralph, Richard, and Mark; and six daughters, Ann, Eleanor, Dorothy, Charlotte, Abigail, and Mary. Thompson had come to the Chignecto Isthmus with a contingent of settlers from Yorkshire in 1774 and was married that same year to Ulster-born Dorothy. They established a farm at Point de Bute, at the head of the Cumberland Basin, where their children were born. Then in 1791, the family journeyed across the isthmus and sailed down the coast to the mouth of River Philip. They travelled upriver to where Black River and Little River flow in, and here they decided to make their home. The following year, Thompson bought 1,500 acres of land from William Allan, who had received a large grant in the area in 1785.

In the 1780s, grants were often made to persons who later subdivided and sold much of their land. Adjacent to the Allan grant was the 2,500-acre grant of Moses Delesdernier, who sold 1,000 acres to John Oxley in 1787. Twelve years later, William Berry purchased 875 acres from Oxley, and in 1802, Berry sold 275 acres to John Ripley. More such complicated transactions took place in the area with purchases and grants. Around the turn of the century, Thompson's neighbours at Oxford included the Oxleys, the Ripleys, and several other families.

The settlers here, like so many others in inland communities of Nova Scotia, made their living by farming and lumbering. The first sawmill was built on the Black River by Richard Thompson, who received a grant of £60 toward its construction. Many other sawmills and gristmills followed, powered by the three rivers that converge in the town. In 1867, Thomas Thompson, William Oxley, John Robb, John G. Wells, and George F. Hewson established the Oxford Manufacturing Company (later the Oxford Woollen Mills) to process wool from the area's sheep. Originally a water-powered carding mill, it employed sixteen workers by 1870. The following year, it was replaced by a larger mill powered by a 25-horsepower steam engine, producing homespun flannels and blankets that were marketed in Saint John and Halifax. The plant was enlarged again in the late 1870s, with a more powerful steam engine, twelve looms, and carding and spinning machines.

Milling was not Oxford's only industry. In 1878, Alex MacPherson, in partnership with I. J. Hingley, established the Oxford Foundry and Machine Company, originally using water power from River Philip. The early years were difficult. The building burned down just two years later and was rebuilt, but the business ran into financial difficulties in 1892. It changed hands again before another fire destroyed it in 1897. It was again rebuilt and expanded, and in the early twentieth century was producing portable sawmills, mining machinery, engines, and mill supplies. The foundry employed thirty people in 1901. It was bought in 1910 by the Wood family, and incorporated as the Oxford

This undated postcard shows one of Oxford's early industries, Oxford Foundry & Machine Co. Ltd. Founded in 1878, the company survived several fires and changes of hands before closing in 1980.

Foundry & Machine Co. Ltd. There was another major fire in the machine shop in 1924, but it was rebuilt yet again on a larger scale. One of its specialties was the Oxford Tram Road Engine, which moved around on wooden tracks and could haul great weights of lumber. Its best years were the 1940s, with improvements made during the Second World War. By 1948, there were forty-three employees. After further changes of ownership, the foundry was torn down in 1980 and replaced by a new business, Oxford Industries Ltd., making machinery and sawmill parts.

The main line of the Intercolonial Railway, linking Halifax with central Canada, had a depot at Oxford Junction, a little to the south of the town, enabling products from the town's industries to be sent to market by rail and allowing goods to be brought in. The Oxford and New Glasgow Railway (known as the "Short Line") opened in 1887, branching off to Stellarton and linking the two industrial areas. By 1900, Oxford had become a busy industrial community at the centre of an important agricultural and lumbering region.

The woollen mill, too, evolved during the course of its existence. In 1903, the old building was replaced by a brick-built mill with new machines, which continued to turn out high-quality cloth that won awards in international exhibitions. In 1908, a sewing department was added, manufacturing men's clothing. During the Second World War, the factory kept busy producing khaki cloth for military uniforms as well as service blankets. After the war, demand for woollens and tweeds declined with changing fashions and synthetic fabrics became popular. The mill closed in 1953. The company was liquidated in 1961, and the building has been repurposed as part of the Cumberland County Exhibition premises.

The second half of the twentieth century brought a new industry to Oxford, reviving the economy as the earlier industries closed. The area around Oxford is blueberry country, and in 1968 John Bragg opened a wild-blueberry processing plant in the town and purchased large tracts of blueberry-growing land. The business flourished, harvesting increased in step with sales of blueberries, and the company has grown from a small enterprise to the world's largest supplier of frozen wild blueberries. Today, the community is home to the headquarters of Oxford Frozen Foods, which is the town's chief employer. With additional blueberry farms in New Brunswick and Maine, the company's two plants can process over three million pounds of berries each day in the peak harvest season. Some of the berries are packaged for immediate use, while many others are frozen for sale out of season and exported around the world. After the blueberry season, the processing plant is kept busy with other products, including frozen carrots, onion rings, and appetizers. The business also includes frozen storage facilities for over 150 million pounds of produce, and a laboratory to ensure quality.

The span of Oxford's history is represented by two structures in the town: a monument to its founder, Richard Thompson, stands behind the United Church, and a huge Blueberry Man on Main Street greets visitors to the town. An annual festival celebrates the central part the blueberry has come to play in the community's prosperity.

A recent event drew a lot of interest from people who had previously known nothing about Oxford. The town lies in an area of what is known as karst topography, where soluble underlying rock is gradually worn away by channels of water below the surface, creating underground caverns which can grow to a considerable size. In July and early August 2018 an area of subsidence was noted in the parking lot of a park maintained by the Lions Club, and truckloads of shale were brought to level the surface. On August 20, the ground suddenly collapsed into the cavern beneath, and a sinkhole formed that was a few metres wide. For days after that, the public watched, fascinated, as the sinkhole continued to grow, so that by early September it had extended to an area of about thirty by forty metres. The park and clubhouse had to be closed, and concern mounted that the subsidence could damage the nearby Trans-Canada Highway. The hole eventually ceased to expand, but the park was no longer viable and the clubhouse was unusable. In 2020, the site was bought, the hole filled in, and at last report the owner was hoping to renovate the property and reopen the park. A new chapter of resiliency is being added to Oxford's history.

Afterword

As I worked on this book, one thing that stood out for me was the incredibly hard work it took to create many of the province's original inland communities. Having left their homes, the newcomers were starting again from scratch in a strange environment. It is hard to imagine the labour it took to create a subsistence farm from virgin forest. The natural vegetation in the interior of the province was dense forest, inhabited by the Mi'kmaq, from whom settlers learned many survival skills. Pioneers making their way inland were faced with the daunting initial task of cutting down trees to create a small clearing in which to build a log cabin for shelter. This work, and the cutting of trails between settlements, had to be done by hand, as did the cultivation of the soil once a clearing had been established.

Although most immigrants brought here under the aegis of the English government were given provisions to help them over the initial settlement period, they needed to grow crops in order eventually to become self-sufficient. The Mi'kmaq were a people living primarily from fishing, hunting, and gathering, but the European settlers came from agricultural societies. Communities developed as neighbours came together to help one another build a house or a barn, or harvest a crop of wheat or oats. In the absence of doctors, women tended the sick and delivered their neighbours' babies. The forest would eventually provide a source of income, but before mechanization, logging was heavy and dangerous physical labour. Without roads in the early days, supplies had to be brought in by boat or hauled over rough trails.

It is not surprising that some of the early inland settlers gave up after a short time, overwhelmed by premature deaths, injuries, and failed crops. Indeed, at first glance it is amazing that so many people remained to create new communities. But having taken the decision to leave their homes and seek their fortunes—or at least survival—in a new land, most of them had little option. As time went on, life became easier: water power from brooks and rivers drove sawmills that enabled the settlers to produce lumber for sale, and gristmills relieved the tedious labour of grinding cereals in stone querns. Fields were cleared for agriculture, and roads were built allowing wagons to take surplus produce to market. Merchants brought in goods, and blacksmiths, carpenters, and other tradesmen joined the communities. Schools and churches were built, and teachers, clergy, and other professionals served the population. Beginning with the natural resources of wood and waterways, the communities' economies developed, and their fortunes rose and fell over time. Their stories, preserved by local historical societies, reflect the arduous labour of the pioneers.

Also, as I was writing I began to realize how much British colonial attitudes had impacted the stories of these communities. They were created by the hard work of their founders, but at the expense of the Indigenous inhabitants of Mi'kma'ki, whose established communities were very different from those of the settlers. Inland settlement encroached on First Nations' hunting grounds, displacing them and impeding their access to traditional sources of food. The reserves that were eventually set up by the colonial government in the guise of compensation—but which in effect were a form of control—reduced many Mi'kmaq to poverty and starvation. Societies that had evolved to use the land and the waterways freely in accordance with the seasons found themselves limited to artificial boundaries that bore no relationship to the availability of game and fishing. And, in step with a policy imposed across the country, Canada's new rulers sent the Mi'kmaw children to a Roman Catholic residential school in Shubenacadie where, along with the trauma of separation from their families, they suffered terrible cruelty and were deliberately deprived of their culture and their language.

Colonial officials in Nova Scotia brought with them the religious prejudices that pervaded politics in Europe: Roman Catholics had been distrusted in England since Tudor days. In the early 1750s, British colonial officials had brought Protestant settlers from regions of Germany, France, and

Switzerland to Nova Scotia to counterbalance both the influence of France and the Catholicism of the Acadians who had been establishing themselves in the area since the 1600s. During the so-called Seven Years War (1756–63) between Britain and France, the Acadians were suspected of disloyalty and consequently deported. Planter communities were established on farmlands behind the dykes created by Acadian labour and ingenuity. The Acadians who returned from exile a couple of decades later found their former homes and fields occupied by English-speaking Protestants.

The Planters were followed by Loyalists who left the United States after the American Revolution, most of whom were white and Protestant. Only later were Catholics—predominately white—welcomed. African Americans who came to Nova Scotia after the American Revolution were either still enslaved by white families or "Free Blacks" who had been promised land, liberty, and provisions for the initial settlement period as a reward for supporting the British during the revolution. In fact, Black settlers were placed in marginal areas, on poor land, with smaller lots than their white counterparts, and without proper title. Provisions were meagre, work was hard to find, and discrimination was rife. Many lived in poverty. Later waves of Black immigrants endured similar treatment.

The bitterness and resentment arising from colonial policies endure to this day. The Acadians have re-established communities that assert their heritage, but they remain vigilant to preserve their language. Indigenous and Black Nova Scotians still suffer discrimination and racial prejudice, although inroads have been made to reclaim their heritage as well. Mi'kmaq History Month in October and Black History Month in February mark occasions when these groups celebrate and share their history and culture. But the colonial policies of the past have influenced the history of our inland communities, and much work still needs to be done to reverse their consequences. This will benefit all of us who live in this beautiful and endlessly diverse province with its complex past—and present.

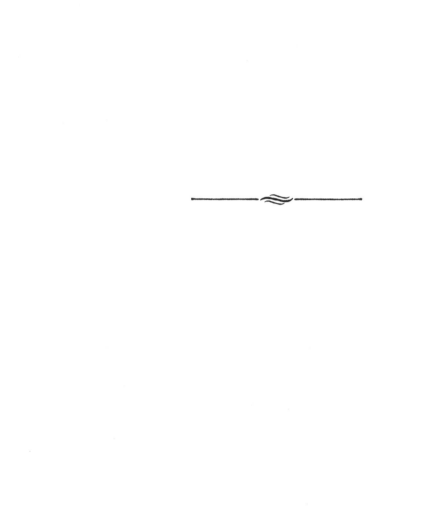

Acknowledgements

*This book was written during the global pandemic, when travel restric-*tions and the closure of many libraries and museums posed challenges to research. I am immensely grateful to the Halifax Central Library, which remained open for much of the past pandemic winter, enabling me to make use of its excellent local history collection, and to its staff for help in locating material. My thanks also to the many volunteers from community historical societies, who have put much valuable material online, and to Wikipedia contributors. And gratitude to the anonymous team at the Nova Scotia Archives who, over the years, have made so many digitized images available to me with a click of a computer mouse. The geniuses who invented Google Street View allowed me to see again places that I was unable to revisit in person. Without these electronic sources, this book could not have been written. Any errors in interpretation are my own.

Thanks to Carol Morrison for sharing her memories of the Oakfield estate, to Sara Beanlands for bringing Fred Veith's fisheries report to my attention, and to Ellen Lewis of the King's County Museum for her help. Special thanks to Heather Laskey for her encouragement and for her valuable suggestions when I was uncertain how to proceed. To my friend Doris Wentzell, a willing and congenial travelling companion, and my son Robert Dawson, for support, advice, and for driving to distant destinations.

Thanks to my editor, Paula Sarson, for problem-solving and bringing it all together, and to Whitney Moran, Angela Mombourquette, and the rest of the team at Nimbus for entrusting me with yet another book. Thanks also to Heather Bryan for creating the map at the beginning of this book, and to Dan Soucoup for dipping into his postcard collection for the cover picture and other images. The help and support of all these people warms my heart.

Bibliography

PRINCIPAL SOURCES

The multi-volume *Dictionary of Canadian Biography*, available online, has been a valuable source of much information about individuals. Ambrose Church's series of topographical county maps, issued between 1865 and 1888, and available at the Nova Scotia Archives, provide details about the state of communities and their economy in the latter part of the nineteenth century. Mi'kmaw place names have, where possible, been taken from the *Mi'kmaw Place Names Digital Atlas*.

BOOKS AND ARTICLES

Anonymous. *Celebration of the 100th Anniversary of the Settlement of Stewiacke! Held on October 6th, 1880.* Truro, NS: The Guardian newspaper & Job Printing Office, 1880.

Candow, James E., ed. *Industry and Society in Nova Scotia: An Illustrated History.* Halifax: Fernwood Publishing, 2001.

Clark, Andrew Hill. *Acadia: The Geography of Early Nova Scotia.* Madison: University of Wisconsin Press, 1968.

Coward, Elizabeth Ruggles. *A History of Bridgetown.* Kentville: n.p., 1955.

Cuthbertson, Brian. *The Old Attorney General: A Biography of Richard John Uniacke.* Halifax: Nimbus Publishing, n.d.

Dawson, Joan. *Nova Scotia's Lost Highways*. Halifax: Nimbus Publishing, 2009.

———. *Nova Scotia's Lost Communities*. Halifax: Nimbus Publishing, 2018.

DesBrisay, Mather Byles. *History of the County of Lunenburg*. 2nd ed., Toronto: William Briggs, 1895.

Furlong, Pauline. *Historic Amherst*. Halifax: Nimbus Publishing, 2001.

Haliburton, Thomas Chandler. *An Historical and Statistical Account of Nova-Scotia: In Two Volumes*. Halifax: J. Howe, 1829.

Harvey, Robert Paton. *Historic Sackville*. Halifax: Nimbus Publishing, 2002.

Howe, Joseph. *Western and Eastern Rambles*, ed. M. G. Parks. Toronto: University of Toronto Press, 1973.

Lescarbot, Marc. *Nova Francia: A Description of Acadia, 1606*, translated by P. Erondelle, 1609. New York: Harper & Brothers, 1928.

MacKay, Donald. *Scotland Farewell: The People of the* Hector. Toronto: McGraw-Hill Ryerson, 1980.

Mennel, Robert M. *Testimonies and Secrets: The Story of a Nova Scotia Family, 1844–1977*. Toronto: University of Toronto Press, 2013.

Nicholson, John A., et al. *Middle River Past and Present: History of a Cape Breton Community*. Middle River Area Historical Society, 1985.

More, James F. *The History of Queens County N.S.* Halifax: Nova Scotia Printing Company, 1873.

Moreira, William, Norm Green, and Tom Sheppard. *Keji: A Guide to Kejimkujik National Park and National Historic Site*. Halifax: Nimbus Publishing, 2005.

Morse, William Inglis. *Local History of Paradise Annapolis County Nova Scotia (1684–1936)*. Boston: Nathan Sawyer & Son, Inc. 1937.

Paine, Albert Bigelow. *The Tent Dwellers: Sports Fishing in Nova Scotia in 1908*. Halifax: Nimbus Publishing Ltd., 2009. First published 1908 by Outing Publishing (New York).

Paul, Daniel N. *We Were Not the Savages: Collision Between European and Native American Civilizations*. 3rd ed. Halifax: Fernwood, 2006.

Robertson, Barbara R. *Sawpower: Making Lumber in the Sawmills of Nova Scotia*. Halifax: Nimbus Publishing and the Nova Scotia Museum, 1986.

Sable, Trudy, and Bernie Francis. *The Language of this Land, Mi'kma'ki*. Sydney, NS: Cape Breton University Press, 2012.

Sandburg, L. Anders, and Deborah Trask. "The Glassworkers of Pictou County, Nova Scotia," *Nova Scotia Historical Review* vol. 11, no. 1. (1991).

Sheppard, Tom. *Historic Bridgewater.* Halifax: Nimbus Publishing, 2008.

———. *Historic Queens County Nova Scotia.* Halifax: Nimbus Publishing, 2001.

Smith, C. Leone. *History of Caledonia, Queens County, Nova Scotia 1820–1973.* Liverpool: Queens County Historical Society, 1997.

Sutherland, George R. *The Rise and Decline of the Earltown Community, 1813–1970.* Truro, Colchester Historical Museum, 1980.

Tennyson, Brian, and Wilma Stewart-White. *Historic Mahone Bay.* Halifax: Nimbus Publishing, 2006.

Trask, Deborah. "The Edward Ross Diaries." *Journal of the Royal Nova Scotia Historical Society* vol. 9 (2006).

Veith, Fred H. O. *Report Upon the Condition of the Rivers in Nova Scotia in Connection with the Fisheries in that Province.* Ottawa: Maclean, Roger & Co., 1884.

Whitelaw, Marjory, ed. *The Dalhousie Journals*, vols. 1 and 2. Ottawa: Oberon Press, 1978, 1981.

Wilson, Alan. *Highland Shepherd: James MacGregor, Father of the Scottish Enlightenment in Nova Scotia.* Toronto: University of Toronto Press, 2015.

ONLINE SOURCES

Bear River, Nova Scotia: Life in a Small Town (blog). "Historic Sketch of Bear River, 1893." bearrivernovascotia.wordpress.com/stories-from-the-past-bear-river-history/historic-sketch-of-bear-river-1893/.

Black Loyalists. "Our History, Our People." blackloyalist.com/cdc/communities/preston.htm.

Canada's Historic Places. "Lock #5, Shubenacadie Canal." historicplaces.ca/en/rep-reg/place-lieu.aspx?id=1788.

Council of Nova Scotia Archives. "Annapolis Valley Macdonald Museum, Middleton."
    archives.novascotia.ca/communityalbums/middleton/.
Cumberland County Genealogical Society. "Wentworth."
    ccgsns.com/local-resources/news-articles-2/wentworth-news-articles/.
Dictionary of Canadian Biography. "DesBarres, Joseph Frederick Wallet."
    biographi.ca/en/bio/desbarres_joseph_frederick_wallet_6E.html.
Fortier, Margaret. "The Cultural Landscape of 18th Century Louisbourg."
    krausehouse.ca/krause/FortressOfLouisbourgResearchWeb/Search/
    MicroRS83_16.html.
Hammonds Plains Historical Society. "Hammonds Plains—A traditional Lumbering Community: A History."
    hammondsplainshistoricalsociety.ca/wp-content/uploads/2012/08/
    History-of-Hammonds-Plains-Area.pdf.
"History of Middle Musquodoboit." sites.rootsweb.com/~nsmusquo/centre_
    musquodoboit/middlemusq.txt.
MacDougall, J. L. Electric Scotland. "History of Inverness County Nova Scotia." electricscotland.com/canada/inverness/index.htm.
Mi'kmaw Place Names Digital Atlas.
    placenames.mapdev.ca/.
New Germany Area Promotion Society. "History of New Germany, Nova Scotia." newgermanycap.ednet.ns.ca/.
Nova Muse. "Oxford Foundry and Machine Company."
    novamuse.ca/Detail/entities/51893.
Nova Muse. "Oxford Manufacturing Company."
    novamuse.ca/Detail/entities/51900.
Nova Scotia Railway Heritage Society. "Wentworth: Then and Now."
    novascotiarailwayheritage.com/files/Wentworth%20brochure-1.pdf.
Paradise Historical Society. "The Paradise Academy."
    paradisehistoricalsociety.ca/paradise-history-the-paradise-academy/.
Parks Canada. "Kejimkujik National Historic site of Canada."
    pc.gc.ca/apps/dfhd/page_nhs_eng.aspx?id=831.
Saltwire. "Ed Coleman's History: The Irish Started the Town of Kentville."
    saltwire.com/opinion/ed-colemans-history-the-irish-started-the-town-of-
    kentville-72232/?location=nova-scotia.

Saltwire. "Everything You Watched in the 1960s and 70s Came through Mill Village, Nova Scotia." saltwire.com/prince-edward-island/lifestyles/everything-you-watched-in-the-1960s-and-70s-came-through-mill-village-nova-scotia-3083/.

Sherbrooke Village. "History of Sherbrooke Village." sherbrookevillage.novascotia.ca/sites/default/files/inline/documents/history_of_sherbrooke_village.pdf.

Sutherland, Ashley. Historic Nova Scotia. "Acadia Mines." historicnovascotia.ca/items/show/114.

Tin Shop Museum. "History of Shubenacadie NS." sites.google.com/site/tinshopmuseumshubenacadiens/history-of-shubenacadie-ns.

Town of Bridgewater. "Our Built Heritage." bridgewater.ca/heritage/heritage-homes/built-heritage-in-bridgewater.

Town of Bridgewater. "Town History and Background, Bridgewater." bridgewater.ca/our-town/visitor-information6/info/town-history.

Town of Middleton: Heart of the Valley. "History of the Town." discovermiddleton.ca/living/history.

Wikipedia. "Joseph Frederick Wallet DesBarres." en.wikipedia.org/wiki/Joseph_Frederick_Wallet_DesBarres#Castle_Frederick.

Wikipedia. "Oakfield, Nova Scotia." en.wikipedia.org/wiki/Oakfield,_Nova_Scotia.

Wikipedia. "Wellington, Nova Scotia." en.wikipedia.org/wiki/Wellington,_Nova_Scotia#History.

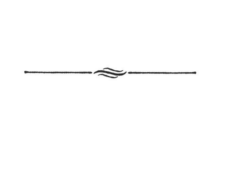

Image Credits

Annapolis Valley Macdonald Museum: 135
Beaton Institute, Cape Breton University: 77
Dawson, Joan: 40, 86, 91, 104, 149, 158
DesBrisay Museum: 132
Library and Archives Canada: 25
Nova Scotia Archives: 12, 16, 21, 30, 35, 45, 50, 55, 59, 64, 68, 72, 82, 98, 109, 122, 125, 141, 153, 163, 168, 173, 177
Nova Scotia Musem: 112, 119
Oxford Historical Society: 180
Soucoup, Dan: cover, ix, xii, 92, 144

ALSO BY JOAN DAWSON

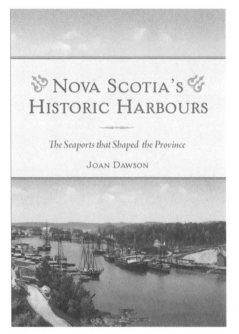

ISBN: 978-1-77108-858-9

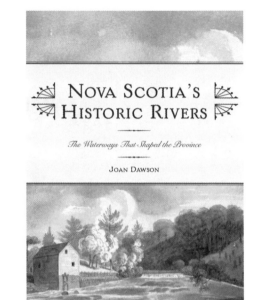

ISBN: 978-1-55109-932-3

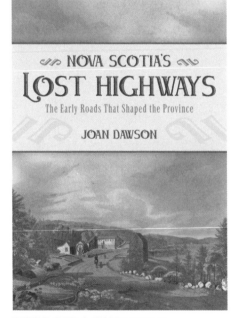

ISBN: 978-1-55109-732-9

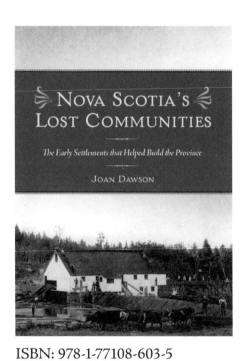

ISBN: 978-1-77108-603-5

*Available at fine bookstores and online
at nimbus.ca*